5.5.94 The day after my first a
on the water....

GW00733035

This is
COMPLETE WINDSURFING

Translated by Barbara Webb

ULRICH STANCIU

This is
COMPLETE WINDSURFING

NAUTICAL

ISBN 0 85177 391 5

First published in Great Britain 1986 by
NAUTICAL BOOKS
an imprint of Conway Maritime Press Ltd.,
24 Bride Lane, Fleet Street,
London EC4Y 8DR.

Typeset by
MJL Typesetting Services Ltd, Hitchin

Printed in Italy

Translated from the German by
Barbara Webb

Photographs by Uli Cop (1), Heike
Dusswald (2), Michael Garff (2), Mike
Harker (10), Dominique Merz (1),
Arnaud de Rosnay (1), Jonathan
Weston (1); all others by Ulli Seer and
the author. Title page photograph by
Patrick Roach.

Contents

Publisher's note

The "This is . . ." series of books covers sailing and boating in full colour wide format. There are several titles on windsurfing. *This is Surfboard Sailing* by Reinhart Winkler and Ulrich Stanciu was first published in 1979, is now out of print and *This is Complete Windsurfing* replaces that early book. *This is Windsurfing* was a paperback edition (Fontana Paperbacks) of *This is Surfboard Sailing. This is Freestyle Windsurfing* by Peter van Wagensveld was published in 1982, followed by *Sailboard Racing* by Rainer Gutjahr. A book essentially for beginners using the latest techniques is *This is Board Sailing* by Uwe Farke, Volker Mohle and Detlef Schroeder (1984). All these titles which originate from United Nautical Publishers S.A., have been published in Great Britain by Nautical Books, now an imprint of Conway Maritime Press.

How boardsailing became one of Europe's favourite sports

'Boardsailing will become more popular than skiing.' This pronouncement by a German sailboard school owner would a few years ago have been received with a weary smile. Europe simply doesn't have the room for several million sailboards, said the disbelievers. And besides, the weather is too cold. But since then the sceptics have learnt to keep quiet. And optimists in the trade reckon that within a decade boardsailing will become one of the most popular single-participant sports in the world.

How has boardsailing managed this extraordinary boom? Because, quite simply, it offers more advantages and fewer disadvantages than other sports.

In the beginning the enthusiasts were looked upon as 'budget sailors', a sort of marine moped rider, figures of fun on their strange boards. But this disparagement has given way to a modest respect: boardsailors are no longer regarded as pitiable screwballs who keep falling into the water, but are often acknowledged experts tearing across the water at unbelievable speed

and getting full enjoyment out of the sport. And it is probably this special blend of the somewhat comical learner and the star quality of the expert which gives boardsailing its cachet.

But it is not just how boardsailing appears to other people that has made it so popular. Everyone who takes it up has a different reason for making it his or her sport — its simplicity, its practicality, its cheapness. Above all, it is easy to learn; a single weekend at a boardsailing school will teach you enough to be able to handle a board on any point of sailing in winds of up to Force 2. Anyone can learn how, at any age; it is a sport that does not require great strength so much as the right technique.

You can go boardsailing anywhere, on the smallest gravel pit or reservoir, on a river, lake or sea; you don't need a mooring place; you can sail on one stretch of water one day, on another the next — your board is always at hand. Transport presents no problems as long as you have access to a car.

Boardsailing is cheap, relatively

speaking. A complete outfit will cost you less than £500. That is quite a lot of money for a young person, but a lot less than you would pay to start skiing. The wind is free, and will always remain so.

The usual rule seems to be that the more excitement a sport offers, the more dangerous it is. This is not true of boardsailing; of course, there is a chance of your being injured, but most injuries are pretty minor ones. A fall lands you in the water, which doesn't hurt.

The fact that boardsailing is one of those 'communing with nature' sports is a major part of its attraction. Nature provides the motive power that draws the boardsailor across the glittering waves in the sunshine. The feeling that you have harnessed this power with your own strength and intelligence is almost intoxicating. The breathtaking sense of speed as you skate over the surface of the water generates emotions that the boardsailor automatically associates with the idea of freedom.

Freedom, for a short time at least, from worry and stress. A boardsailor is so preoccupied with his own balance and with the trim of the sail that he has no time to think of anything else. Freedom, too, to decide just where you want to go; whether to go fast or slow. On a sailboard everyone is his own captain.

Boardsailing is also a healthy sport that does the body good, even if it imposes quite heavy loads on certain muscles. It has the advantage of being a sport that doesn't exclude the family — you always leave from the same point on the beach, and the children will enjoy playing on the board when it is not in use.

Environmentalists won't find anything to criticise in the sport. The environment only suffers when sailors drop their litter on the beach or stray into nature reserves. The sport itself pollutes neither water nor air, is not noisy and leaves behind no marks on the landscape — by nightfall all the coloured sails have vanished from the foreshore.

All these practical reasons, together with the sheer exhilaration of board-sailing, give adherents of the sport a real feeling of achievement, a sort of fever that never goes away. Occasional boardsailors can very quickly become fanatics who spend most of their free time on the water. Nor does the sense of achievement ever diminish: even after you have become an expert there are always more difficult conditions or locations to try. There is always another mountain to climb.

Boardsailing offers a wide range of possibilities. You can sail in light winds, strong wings or surf; you can concentrate on trick sailing, cruising or racing. Competition presents the greatest challenge, because it is not just a question of mastering the techniques, but also of using your brain. The rules are complex, and tactics demand a good grasp of physics, aerodynamics, meteorology and psychology. Racing is rather like waterborne chess.

Finally, the sport offers you the chance to meet other people with similar interests everywhere — on the water, on the beach, in the club or in the bar — people for whom the most important thing in life is not money, but which way and how strongly the wind is blowing.

Of course, with so many pluses there have to be a few minuses. To a beginner especially, these may appear significant; boards may be cheaper than sailing dinghies, but they are still expensive — in particular, as we said, for the young. They are also difficult to store in small flats. You can never be certain that the weekend will bring the right wind. And then there are the minor fears — of falling into the water, getting cold, injuring yourself, or of being unable to control the board and finding yourself suddenly in danger.

But forewarned is forearmed, as they say. This book aims to teach you all the secrets of boardsailing in every one of its variations, to guide and advise you, so that you make the graduation from novice to expert as easily, as fast and as enjoyably as possible.

PART I:
BOARDSAILING FOR BEGINNERS

Where to learn

Of course, you don't have to go to a school to learn boardsailing. It's a sport that can be taught by a friend, a relation, a husband or a wife; which means that you don't pay any course fees and that you're free to head for the water whenever you have time, inclination and a suitable wind. The equipment, too, including board and wet suit, can be borrowed — and you're ready to go.

But there are drawbacks to being taught by an amateur, however good he or she is at boardsailing. They may not have a gift for teaching, or the patience not only to pass on the techniques to a pupil but also to awake in him or her the passion for boardsailing that comes with success. Often this kind of arrangement ends with both sides feeling frustrated and irritated and the pupil losing the desire to learn.

The help you will get from a professional instructor, on the other hand, is surer, more successful, more

Many schools used a simulator for the early learning stages before going afloat.

entertaining and in the end probably cheaper. Not only will the instructor have special equipment to help you learn (such as a simulator), but he or she will also be trained in the art of instruction. An expert boardsailor who knows all the techniques, your instructor will also be best placed to give you impartial advice and prevent you making expensive mistakes when you come to buy your first board.

At a school a beginner has a chance to find out whether boardsailing is for him or not before committing himself to the expense of a board, wet suit, boots and so on. Have a trial lesson before embarking on a full course, and check out the quality of the instruction and the standard of equipment at the school. As a rule, theory and practice are spread over ten lessons. The pupil-teacher ratio on the water should be no greater than seven to one.

There are thus several advantages to learning boardsailing in a school:

● Safety when learning — the pupil is constantly supervised and helped if he gets into difficulties.

● Safety later — he will be made aware of safety (Rule of the Road) and taught how to anticipate bad weather and cope with emergencies.

● Faster learning, as the instructor will be an experienced teacher who is able to make a competent board-sailor out of the average pupil in some seven to ten lessons.

● More enjoyable learning, because a school gives the pupil a chance to meet other people and to realise that the difficulties he is experiencing are common to all beginners.

● The instructor can anticipate and therefore prevent some of the typical beginner's mistakes.

● No setting-up costs — learning in a school gives the pupil a chance to discover whether he likes boardsailing enough to invest in the necessary equipment. He can also try out several different sailboards and find out which type suits him best.

● Occasionally a hirer will ask for some evidence of ability, such as a course completion certificate, before allowing you to borrow one of his boards.

The following bodies will send out free information about boardsailing and a list of recommended schools: Royal Yachting Association, 1 Victoria Way, Woking, Surrey. Tel: 04862 5022.
Association of Professional Boardsailing Centres, Whitewater Sports, Shepperton Marina, Felix Lane, Shepperton, Middlesex. Tel: 0932 225988.

All in all, we recommend that you do take some professional instruction. This book is designed as an adjunct to that tuition: to help you not only with useful additional information during the course but later on, at home or on windless days on the beach, with answers to any questions you may have about boardsailing.

We hope you have fun...

Where to learn

The ideal practice ground

Boardsailing is an independent sport. You are not tied to special areas by the need for expensive launching facilities or fixed moorings. With the board on the roof of your car you can simply head off for the stretch of water you want and which is most suited to your ability. The only facilities needed are somewhere to park, preferably not too far from the water, and a place near the water's edge where you can rig and unrig the board undisturbed.

There are, of course, some places where watersports are not allowed — nature reserves or bathing areas, commercial harbours, marinas and their approaches — and where boardsailing is similarly proscribed. Also there are places which are restricted to a certain type of water sport, such as water skiing.

Ideally you should acquaint yourself with the facts before trying out a new patch, as the use of some waters is subject to certain conditions: there may be a launch fee to pay, or you may have to comply with regulations limiting your sailing to a minimum distance from the shore, or you may have to use a special channel to launch and leave the shore.

But even more important is to make sure that you are aware of local conditions that may affect your safety. Find out about the currents in inland waters, the tides on coastal waters, the shallows (sandbanks, rocks or wrecks) and so on.

If you take these precautions you will avoid risking your safety and damaging your equipment. Boardsailing is only dangerous if you ignore the idiosyncrasies of different stretches of water.

Most of this information will be available in local guidebooks, on notice boards or from the police. But you may be fairly sure it's safe if you see a lot of people sailing on the water already.

The ideal venue for a beginner is a wide, sandy beach leading down gently into the water, with no groynes, few swimmers, breakwaters, stones or rocks. Sand or fine shingle is best, because the beginner who has not yet mastered steering will save himself and his board a lot of pain if he ensures a soft landing.

Do, always, stay well clear of swimmers or stretches of beach with lots of bathers. If you drop the sail, the

Wind blowing along the shore, a sandy beach and calm water close in provide the ideal conditions for learning.

falling mast can seriously injure a swimmer; when you are just beginning you will have little control over your board, and accidental falls will be common. If there are one or two bathers in the vicinity, keep at least ten yards between you and them.

It is important that the water be the right depth. Hip or chest-deep water, shelving gently down from the shore, is ideal, because you can climb back on board after a fall easily and without wasting energy. Also, if you get into trouble, you need only hop off and push or pull your board ashore.

For the beginner, smaller lakes, gravel pits and reservoirs have the twin advantages of permitting supervision and ensuring that you can always reach the bank somewhere and walk back to your departure point. Try to stay close to the bank within shouting distance. Find a quiet corner where you can get on with your first exercises undisturbed.

If you have to learn on a larger lake or on coastal waters, make sure that there are no waves. At the beginning you need absolutely calm water to develop your sense of balance; waves will make practising doubly difficult. But even on calm water never go out of hailing distance from the shore.

Shallow water, such as on a lake, helps you learn quicker since you can climb back on the board more easily.

The ideal beginner's wind

It might be that you are faced with flat, relatively calm water just beyond the shoreline but a stiff breeze blowing. This typically happens with an offshore wind, in other words a wind that is blowing from the land directly out over the water.

The wind is 'blanketed' and diverted by every obstacle in its path — trees, houses, hills — as it approaches the shore, and since it takes some distance for the waves to build up there will be an area of calm water close inshore, with both wind and waves gradually increasing as you move further out. There is a *very real danger* with this type of wind that every time you fall, every time you raise sail again, you will be carried further from the beach. Even experienced sailors can underestimate the danger.

It is therefore *imperative* to establish first which way the wind is blowing, and only go afloat in an offshore wind when there is land downwind on to which you will be driven.

On the coast an offshore wind is especially dangerous. Only when you have fully mastered boardsailing should you think of putting to sea in such conditions — and then take great care to remain close inshore.

A wind blowing directly on to the beach, in other words an onshore wind, presents no such dangers. If you fall off you will be carried towards the shore rather than away from it. Unfortunately, you will have to contend with rougher water, because on any stretch of water larger than a small lake the wind will have had the space in which to build waves.

The ideal beginner's wind is therefore one blowing along the shore — whether from left or right makes no difference.

How do you find out which way the wind is blowing? Simple: the old tricks — throw a couple of blades of grass in the air; or wet a finger, hold it up, and the side that feels colder will be the windward one. You could also watch the trees to see which way they are bending; the small flags, or burgees, at the masthead of other sailing boats; or flags flying on land. They will all indicate where the wind is blowing from. Take note of the direction.

The most accurate wind indicator is actually your own sail, and you will soon develop a nose for the wind and find the knowledge coming almost automatically.

A few words about wind strength. Your first attempts should be in a light breeze of no more than Force 3 on the Beaufort scale.

Force 1: light airs, sea calm
Force 2: light breeze, sea ruffled
Force 3: gentle breeze, small wavelets

Practising in a flat calm, or a wind of less than Force 1, is not recommended. You always need some wind pressure on the sail in order to keep your balance, to steer the board and, of course, to make forward progress.

For the beginner warm, sunny weather with a water temperature of over 18 degrees C (64°F) is best. This will make even accidental falls fun. Also take the time and trouble to find

A wetted finger will tell you where the wind is: the cold side is the windward one.

Your own sail is the best indicator of wind direction: the clew always points to leeward, directly away from the wind.

yourself a spot where both wind and water are right. Treat your practising like a game; keep telling yourself that you're just going swimming and that you're taking along a bath toy in the shape of your board. And when you fall in, don't let it worry you — it's no more significant than jumping into the water from the side of a swimming pool. Falling in is all part of the game — anyone who doesn't fall will never be a good boardsailor.

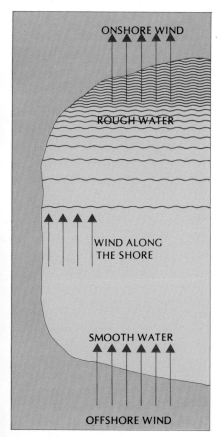

Be careful never to practise in an offshore wind. An onshore wind is better, but brings with it higher waves. The ideal conditions are a wind blowing parallel to the shore.

The wind strength can be accurately gauged from the sea state; if the waves are developing crests, the wind is too strong for novices.

The right equipment

For nine out of ten beginners — whether they have been to boardsailing school or not — one thought is uppermost: they must have their own board. This brings in its train a whole series of questions: Which board to buy? What type of rig is sensible? What extras are needed? And what should the whole thing cost?

To get the ideal kit to suit your requirements, your ability, your ambitions and your pocket, you will need a basic minimum of knowledge about the construction of sailboards, the materials used and the composition of your equipment.

On page 20 you will find further information and tips on what to look for when buying a board.

Another advantage of boardsailing: the full kit consists of only seven items and can be built up very quickly.

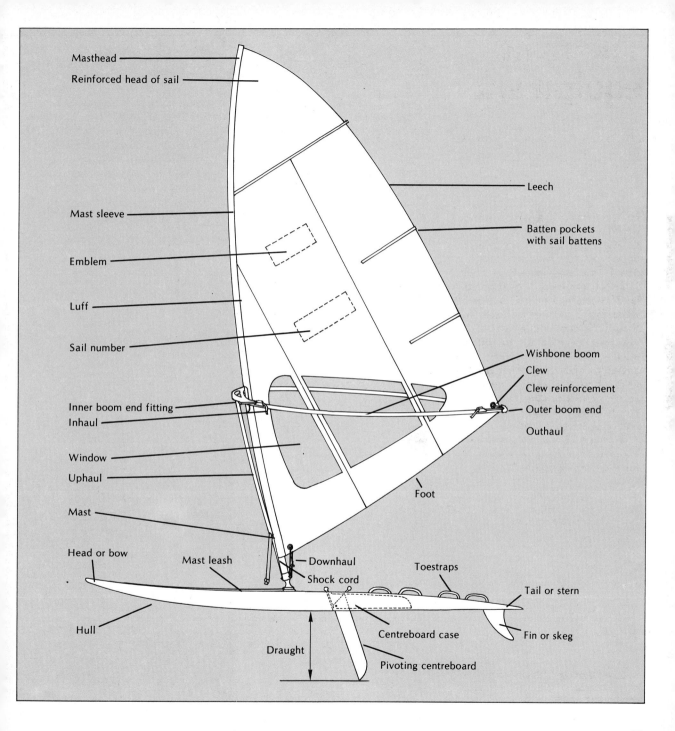

Masthead
Reinforced head of sail
Mast sleeve
Emblem
Luff
Sail number
Inner boom end fitting
Inhaul
Window
Uphaul
Mast
Head or bow
Hull
Leech
Batten pockets
with sail battens
Wishbone boom
Clew
Clew reinforcement
Outer boom end
Outhaul
Foot
Mast leash
Downhaul
Shock cord
Toestraps
Tail or stern
Centreboard case
Fin or skeg
Draught
Pivoting centreboard

The ideal beginner's board

The choice of models available is vast. To bring some order into the confusion, there are four basic categories of board:

Allround board
Race board
Allround funboard
Funboard

Needless to say, this distinction is not rigid, as there are many boards which straddle the border between one and the next group.

While in the case of the extreme boards — racing boards and pure funboards — constructional specifications are now fairly well established, among the allround boards development is still under way. Dual-purpose boards also have competition from a relatively new type of allround board, which gives even the expert a worthwhile ride: the allround funboard. The dimensions, shape and volume of this multi-purpose board place it among the allrounders, but it retains much of the character of the funboard.

In general the conventional allround board is more suited to light winds and inland waters, while the allround funboard is better adapted to strong winds and coastal conditions. More and more types of board are coming onto the market that behave in light winds like middle-of-the-road models but in stronger winds take on some of the attributes of the expert's boards. However, the standard allround is probably the best board to learn on.

The final choice for you will depend

Race board

Allround board

Allround fun board

Funboard

CHARACTERISTICS OF THE BOARDS

	Allround	Race board	Allround funboard	Funboard
Length (m)	over 3.6	3.8-3.9	3.4-3.7	not over 3.5
Volume (litres)	over 210	over 220	over 180	not over 200
Weight (kg)	at least 18	at least 18	about 16	not over 16
Centreboard	Daggerboard or pivoting centreboard	Large dagger-board or pivoting centreboard	Pivoting centreboard	No centreboard or small pivoting centreboard
Footstraps	sometimes	sometimes	yes	yes
Wind (Beaufort)	1-5	1-5	1-6	4-7
Ability	Limited	Proficient	Proficient	Expert

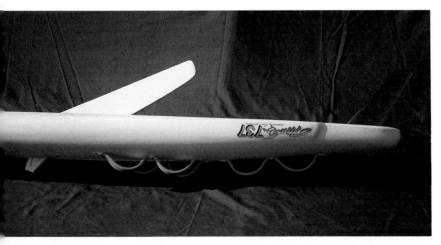

A beginner's board should have a fully retractable centreboard. You can probably dispense with footstraps, at least initially, but you may want to fit them later.

Different forms of fin. The shape helps determine the board's directional stability and responsiveness.

on price, but also on the the following criteria:

Stability: This is the magic ingredient as far as beginners are concerned. Before you learn any sophisticated tricks you will have to be able to stand on the board. The most stable board has a low profile and a flat underhull, because the resistance to the water at the sides is greater with a wide, flat bottom than with a more rounded hull. Maximum beam (of at least 66cm, or 26in) should be at a point somewhere between the centreboard slot and about 50cm (20in) in front of the mast. The low profile gives a lower centre of gravity.

A deep centreboard will help to prevent one or two unintentional swims at the beginning of your board-sailing career. Extending vertically down from the hull, it will serve to damp down any tendency to roll. A fully retractable centreboard is best for the beginner, as your first efforts are likely to take place in shallow water, with consequent risk of occasional grounding, when the centreboard will swing up out of the way.

The internal volume should be relatively large to ensure the buoyancy and stability that the learner needs. A begginer's board should have a capacity of at least 200 to 220 litres so that it doesn't immediately dive when you suddenly shift your weight too far forward or aft. The extra buoyancy provided by the bigger volume also ensures that the board does not react so violently to the usual mistakes that a novice makes.

Other aspects of design and construction that you should watch out for in choosing your first board: it should not be so responsive that incorrect trimming of the rig results in sudden and unexpected turns; it should be directionally stable. It should point up well — in other words, be able to sail close to the wind — as beginners often have difficulty in getting back to their starting point. In no case should it have pronounced weather helm, which is the term for a tendency to round up into wind when the sail is sheeted in hard.

Good directional stability and controlled response will prove an advantage later on when you learn to tack and gybe. The slower a board turns, the greater are your chances of carrying out these first manoeuvres successfully and remaining on the board — sudden and unexpected movements of the board are the main reasons for learners developing an over familiarity with the water too early on...

As far as the material of the board is concerned, there are one or two things you should watch out for. The stronger the material, the better. A board for the first exercises should be made of thermoplastic polyethylene or ABS/ASA. Both of these will merely form the outer covering of a solid core of closed-cell foam that ensures the board will stay afloat even if holed. Later on, when you get onto advanced techniques such as surf sailing, you should never forget that your board will always remain afloat and can always be relied upon to support you whatever the circumstances.

Exactly what is meant by ABS/ASA and polyethylene is explained later on in the book, along with details of other materials in common use.

A beginner's board should on no account have sharp edges or hard protruding parts, so that possible injury when falling is avoided.

Specification of a typical beginner's board
Wide and flat-bottomed for stability
Volume of at least 200 litres for buoyancy
Should point as high as possible
Should be directionally stable
Should on no account be prone to nose diving
Should not carry weather helm

A beginner's board should have a volume of at least 200 litres. This will make raising sail easier.

The basic rig

The rig, in other words the assembly of mast, mast foot, sail and wishbone, is the motor of the sailboard. The bigger the sail area, the more powerful the motor. And in the same way as a fast sports car is totally unsuitable for a novice driver, a large rig is not recommended for the first-time boardsailor. But area is not the only factor in determining whether a particular rig is suitable for the beginner; there are other considerations which can make it easier or more difficult to control.

Some time ago we saw the development of the so-called 'comfort rig'. This was designed to be significantly easier to control on the water, not only for beginners but also for experts in strong winds.

So whether you are a beginner or an advanced sailor you should have a comfort rig in your wardrobe. This is not just easier to use afloat, but is also simpler to rig and dismantle on land. More and more manufacturers seem to be producing rigs that are a puzzle to put together. So it is sensible to check a rig before buying it to see that all the parts fit together and that it is supplied with a set of instructions. 'Comfort' also suggests that you don't need too much strength to assemble all the bits.

Essential for an easy start: the comfort rig, with its high clew and short wishbone boom.

The mast

The first sailboard masts were made of glassfibre (more properly, glass-fibre-reinforced plastic, or GRP). With these, a tapered metal core was covered in several thin layers of glassfibre bound together with resin. This method of manufacture gives a spar with an exceptionally high 'bendability', which is important, because the sail shape is designed to change with the strength of the wind: flat in a strong wind, full in a light breeze.

Most plastic masts nowadays are made of epoxy resin, which will take a higher loading. There are also available medium-hard and hard aluminium masts, which hardly bend at all but which have a very high breaking strain; and carbon fibre masts, which are very light, but are much more expensive than either aluminium or GRP masts.

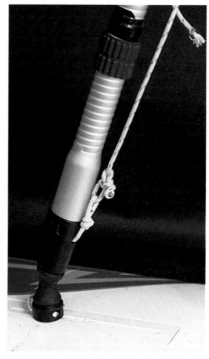

gives enough of a safety margin.

Look closely at the universal joint. Rubber components are best for the UJ, as they are less likely to cause injury than metal and/or plastic joints. The bottom of the joint should fit snugly into the hole in the board and stay there. But if force is needed to get the mast foot into the board, or out again, it is too tight. If, on the other hand, the mast foot fits too loosely, you will later experience problems on the water when you try to raise the rig. The mast foot should fit firmly enough in its socket for you to be able to lift the board with it. Most modern boards are now fitted with sliding mast foot tracks — some

more easily adjustable than others. Make sure the one you choose is simple and well engineered — too complicated ones can clog with sand.

If the mast and boom are allowed to fill up with water they become heavy as lead, and impossible to lift, so it is important that both be made water-tight with plastic stoppers. It is also worth ensuring that the sail does not have a loose-fitting mast sleeve, which would fill up with water upon immersion and make the mast unnecessarily heavy to lift to the point at which the water begins to run out.

The wishbone boom

The boom is about the most important component of a sailboard. Together with the mast, it extends and supports the sail, and you hold the rig up with it. You also use it to steer the board and keep your own balance. The boom should be the right length for the sail. If in due course you start to use a smaller, higher clewed sail it will be worth investing in another, shorter boom, or an adjustable boom.

An important criterion is the stiffness of the boom. If it is too flexible, the two halves will bend away from each other under load, in so doing shortening the effective length of the boom and allowing the sail to belly out. Why this is undesirable, especially in strong winds or in a gust, you will find out in a later chapter.

For this reason it is best to have a somewhat heavy but more solid boom. A good boom will at no point touch the sail. The grip should not be too rough and should be glued firmly round the tube. Grips that are just slid on will twist round and will not last long.

Mast foot and universal joint

A vital part of the rig, which gives the sailboard its pleasure or frustration, is the joint at the foot of the mast. The joint has to keep the mast in place even when the sail is raised out of the water, but must release itself the instant the sailor's leg gets caught between the board and the mast in the case of a fall. The mast foot has to be able to spring out immediately, in the same way as a ski's safety binding gives, before it causes an injury. A release strain of something of the order of 90 to 130lb (40-60kg)

The sail

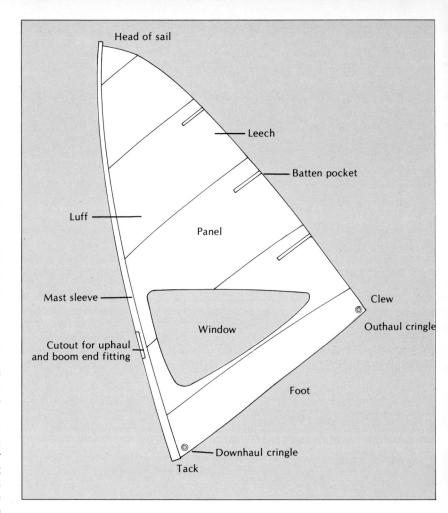

The sail is one of man's oldest forms of engine. Although it had to be adapted for use in the relatively new sport of boardsailing its basic form and function have changed little. Thee are, however, two noticeable differences: a sailboard's sail has a sleeve which is simply pulled over the mast and drawn down; and it is loose-footed.

Modern sails are made of rotproof artificial fibre fabric, usually Dacron or Mylar. The silk-finish or metallic Mylar sails are much lighter and less prone to stretch than the more common Dacron, retaining their shape even under great strain.

Even the most experienced sail-makers differ in their views of the best way to cut a sail. One will opt for 12 panels, another will be content with five; one will bring the panels out to the leech at right angles, while another will prefer vertical or even radial panels. So choosing a sail requires some expertise and experience.

It is important to have a large window for clear visibility in all directions. A sail will be easier to lift out of the water if it has a short boom and a higher clew. The boom should not be longer than 7ft 6in (2.30m), with 6ft 6in (2.00m) giving easier handling. The area of a good comfort rig will lie between 5 and 5.5m² (54-59ft²).

A necessary word about the care of a sailboard sail. From the first moment you use it it will begin to be worn away by the rough sand and the action of the water. A little care will pay handsome dividends in making sure that your sail lasts an extra season or two. Never put it away wet or shove it roughly into a sail bag; leave it spread out for a few minutes to dry in the wind, so that dirt and sand can be simply brushed off.

If you intend to go out again

The standard rig for most boards has a sail area of about six square metres.

shortly, the rig need not be completely dismantled. Release the outhaul, and roll the sail up round the mast. Lay the boom along the mast, tie it all together in a neat bundle, and you will have an easy-to-carry package which can be re-rigged in a

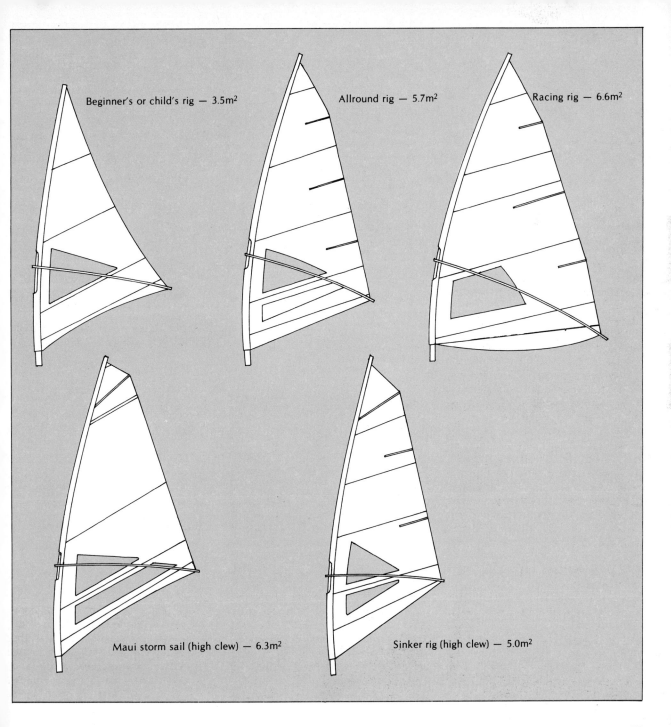

Beginner's or child's rig — 3.5m²

Allround rig — 5.7m²

Racing rig — 6.6m²

Maui storm sail (high clew) — 6.3m²

Sinker rig (high clew) — 5.0m²

minute when you want to go sailing again.

For longer car journeys or breaks between sails you should dismantle the rig completely. Do not fold the sail like a blanket; instead, fold it from the foot upwards, with each fold parallel to the foot so that the mast sleeve forms a zigzag pattern as shown in the picture. You can then either roll it up from the leech or fold it again.

Always check your sail for the slightest signs of wear — for example, to see whether the stitching is coming undone on the batten pockets, the clew cringle is beginning to tear out or the sailcloth is beginning to wear through. Make sure you carry out any such repairs before they cost you a wasted weekend.

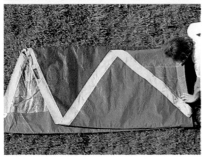

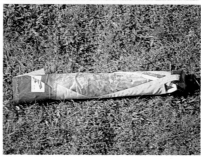

This is the simplest and neatest way to roll up a sail.

The uphaul

The uphaul also repays attention. Only too often these are too short. Ideally the knotted line (knotted for easier grip) should end about 20cm (8in) above the board. The correct length, as with the correct height for the boom, will depend on how tall you are; if you measure more than 6ft (1.80m), you may find you have to add more line for your own comfort.

Mast leash

For your own safety a mast leash, or rig retaining line, is essential. This is a line for the mast foot to the board which prevents the board from drifting away if the rig slips out. In wind of only Force 4 or 5 even a good swimmer will find it difficult to catch up with a drifting board. But if the rig is firmly attached to the board it acts as a sort of sea anchor and holds the board back. The mast leash should be made of line at least 6mm (quarter-inch) in diameter, with a breaking strain of over 100kg (220lb), and should be firmly secured to both board and rig. The attachment points on board and rig should be equally strong.

Vitally important: the mast leash.

Specification of a comfort rig
Sail area: 5 to 5.5m² (54-59ft²)
Wishbone boom: lightweight and short — not longer than 2.30m (7ft 6in)
Sail cut: high clew
Mast: lightweight and watertight
Mast sleeve: not too wide
Mast foot: release load between about 40 and 60kg (90-130lb)
Mast leash: should take a load of at least 100kg (220lb), and should ideally be secured to the bow of the board
Assembly: simple and without the need for great strength.
Follow the instructions carefully.

Don't let yourself become bogged down in technicalities. Keep it simple. Remember, the most important thing, as in any sport, is that your equipment works, and works well. That way you will get maximum enjoyment out of your boardsailing.

The right clothing

Not only your comfort, but also your health depends on what you wear when you go boardsailing. However warm the day may be, the evaporation of spray on wind-blown, wet skin will make you colder faster when out on the water than if you were sunbathing on the beach. Warm, durable clothing will prevent you getting cold, and will also protect you from sunburn and grazes.

The choice of wet suits is as wide as the choice of boards, and the price/quality ratio is even more difficult to determine. But a couple of pointers can be given:

Function: The suit should fit well and be warm. What it looks like is of secondary importance, so don't let yourself be swayed by fashion at the expense of practicality.

Material: Your first suit should be made of neoprene, which is an elastic foam that absorbs water when you fall in. This thin layer of water is then warmed up to body temperature by the adjacent skin and provides you with a protective layer of insulation against the cold outside.

The insulating ability of this material is best at a thickness of about 4mm. Neoprene suits are available single or double-lined. The lining is usually made of nylon. Single-lined material is usually covered only on the inside, with an unprotected neoprene outside. Wet suits of this type are significantly warmer and more elastic than double-lined suits, but more delicate. Which one you choose will depend on your own preference — greater warmth or durability — and is something only you can decide.

For the early- and late-season boardsailor who finds the summer too short, a dry suit is a good idea. This is a light artificial fibre overall that has

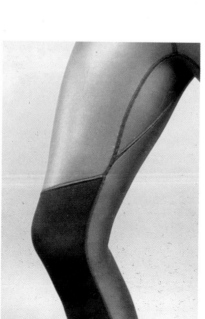

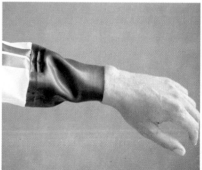

A dry suit that fits tightly at neck and wrists will keep you warm even in winter.

A beginner's wet suit should be reinforced at the knees, which are constantly scratched and scraped by the board.

no warming properties as such. It is so close-fitting at neck, wrists and ankle that you stay dry. You therefore wear normal warm clothing underneath, such as a track suit or skiwear. Nowadays you can also obtain neoprene dry suits and 'steamers', which are good idea for a winter boardsailing.

Cut: Wet suits with legs but without arms, called Long Johns, are usually accompanied by a short bolero top. Depending on the wind and water temperature you can go sailing either with or without the top. Warmer, but not as versatile, is the one-piece suit, which is simply a Long John with arms and collar. You can also buy suits with short legs, called shorties, which are only really suitable for hot summer days.

Fitting: Some suits that fit as if they were made for you when you try them on in the shop subsequently prove to be too loose or too tight. You are at the mercy here of the advice and expertise of the retailer. At hand and foot the suit should fit tightly without constricting. If arms and legs are fitted with zip fasteners to make donning and removal easier, these should be made of plastic, not metal, so that they withstand the effects of sand and salt water.

The weak point of any suit, wet or dry, is its seams, which are usually stitched and glued. Internal seams should not sit proud of the fabric, or they will rub against the skin. The fewer seams a suit has (in others words, the fewer separate panels it comprises), the warmer it will be, as each seam will let in a certain amount of cold water.

Shoes will protect you against injury — for instance, if your ankle is strapped between the foot of the

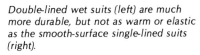

Double-lined wet suits (left) are much more durable, but not as warm or elastic as the smooth-surface single-lined suits (right).

The so-called 'shorties' are only suitable for mid-summer sailing in warm climes. If a strong wind is blowing it is best to wear a full suit.

mast and the board or if you tread on sharp stones or shards of glass on the beach. To begin with it is best to buy a cheap pair of trainers or sailing shoes. Special insulated boardsailing shoes or boots are only worth buying if their surface material is neoprene. As a general rule they should fit well enough to stop your foot slipping forward in them; otherwise your toes will keep being forced up into the toe-cap, which over the long term can be painful. Make sure that the soles of your shoes or boots are non-slip, in other words that they won't slide around on the surface of your board.

If you aren't scared off by the cold water, and intend to sail through the autumn and winter, it is worth investing in a neoprene hood and gloves.

Shoes will not only protect you from cold, but also from injury from glass, stones and sea urchins. A well-designed non-slip sole will give your feet a firmer grip on the board.

A balaclava-type hood is only necessary if you want to sail before April or after October. Gloves are of dubious value; the harder you grip the boom, the more they will tend to restrict circulation in your fingers.

Taking your board to the water

One of the sailboard's main attractions is its mobility, allowing you to store it almost anywhere, to transport it a hundred miles by motorway to the sea or along a country road to the nearest stretch of water. But you should take care that neither board not care are damaged. That is to say, the roof rack you use must be capable of holding the board firmly even under the powerful slipstream caused by high-speed motorway travel; it should not budge, even when braking hard; and on bumpy roads the board should remain locked in place on the roof rack.

The roof rack

A sailboard roof rack differs from the conventional luggage rack in having unusually wide and strong gutter attachments. The bars that support the board should not have sharp edges, and ideally should be covered with some cushioning such as foam or rubber tubing.

If you ever go skiing and have your own equipment, get a roof rack that will also accept skis. The retaining straps should be wide so that they do not damage the board (strong, synthetic webbing is best) and should neither work loose nor wear through. Not every roof rack suits every model of car, so make sure that the one you get is suitable for your vehicle.

The rack should be easy and quick to fit. If fitting it is a long chore, it will spend the whole of the season on the roof. Not only will this put your precious cargo at risk from fittings working loose; it will also cost you more in petrol.

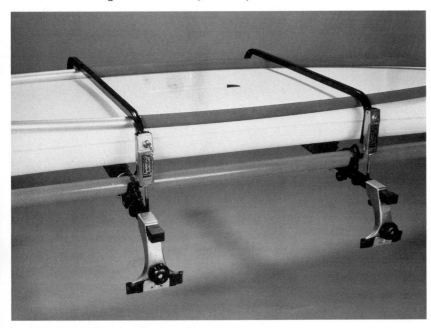

A secure and thiefproof roof rack is a prerequisite if you want to carry your board on the car.

Loading the roof rack

The board should be placed on the roof rack upside down and with the bow facing towards the front of the car, which gives it the most aerodynamic profile for high-speed driving. The retaining strap should not be pulled as tight as possible, as this could buckle the material of the board and impair its performance. Since the straps are liable to stretch, which allows the board to shift it is important that on long journeys or in rain you periodically check them to see that they are still tight and inspect the load to make sure it is still secure.

Depending on the design of the roof rack the wishbone boom will be carried either on top of or underneath the board. The mast must be fixed in a special holder attached to the rack. It is possible to buy a pair of clamps to fix it directly to the rack, but this is less secure and may damage the mast.

Make sure when you are loading up that you do not break the law. The board may extend up to a metre beyond your car, but if so you may be obliged to tie a red marker about a foot square to the stern, or a red light at night.

Driving with the board on the roof

The additional weight and the high roof loading will give your driving a strange feel at first. Overtaking and acceleration will be much slower because of the increased air resistance, while the higher profile will make the car more susceptible to crosswing, and the higher centre of gravity will make itself felt when cornering. Drive more carefully than usual, try to anticipate more, and remember to check the load from time to time.

A simple retaining strap will not deter a thief from making off with your board, so if you are worried about security it may be worth investing in a lockable rack. When choosing one make sure that the mast and boom can also be locked, and always ensure that the clasps are fully engaged before you leave the car.

The right way to carry two boards: wind resistance is least if they are stacked one on top of the other.

Rigging the right way

The most important knots

Knots that everyone uses on land, such as the favourite 'granny knot', are useless on the water. When wet they will either slip or, more usually, lock up solid and become impossible to undo. The boardsailor *must* therefore learn the most important sailor's knots and practise them until he or she can do them blindfold. It is also quite fun to master a few knots which you can then use throughout life. Not for nothing have the ones shown here been used by generations of sailors. Even in soaking wet line they can usually be released easily as soon as the tension is removed.

In boardsailing you will need the following knots:

Figure-of-eight knot

Purpose: Prevents a line from slipping through or out of a cringle or jamming cleat.
Where used: At the free end of the inhaul; at both ends of the clew outhaul; as the first part of the cow hitch (see opposite) and, on some boards, on the uphaul and the mast leash at the foot of the mast.

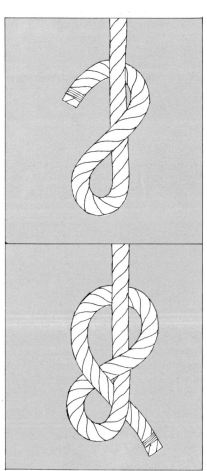

Half hitch

Purpose: Secures the end of a line to a fitting.
Where used: To fasten the downhaul after it has been pulled tight, or as an additional safety measure to secure the free end of the outhaul and inhaul after they have been fastened to the cleat (in place of a figure-of-eight).

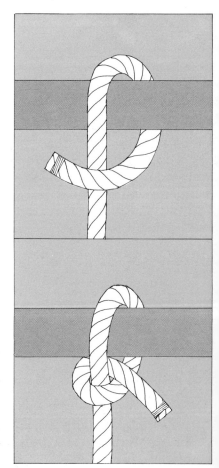

Rolling hitch

Purpose: Secures the end of a line to a round, smooth fitting (such as the mast).
Where used: To fasten the inhaul to the mast.

Cow hitch

Purpose: Same as the rolling hitch. As secure as the rolling hitch, but simpler to make, although it can work loose.
Where used: Same as the rolling hitch.

Bowline

Purpose: Makes a loop that will not slip under load.
Where used: To fasten the downhaul to the sail cringle or to the mast foot, depending on the design; additional fastening for the mast leash to mast foot or through a hole in the board; to form a handhold in the outhaul to tune the sail (especially in competitive boardsailing).

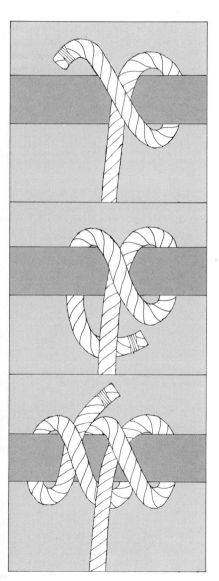

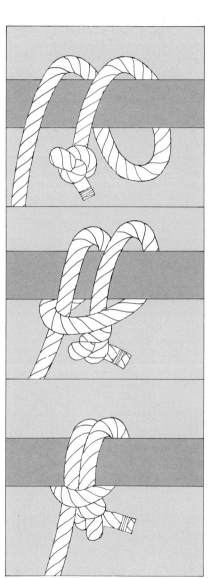

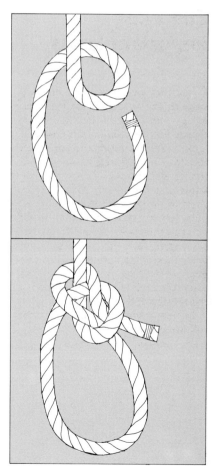

Sheet bend

Purpose: Joins two lines of unequal thickness.

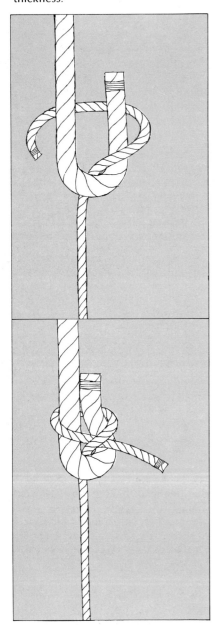

Reef knot

Purpose: Joins two lines of equal thickness.

Assembling the rig

Mastering the knots is the first step to learning how to rig, but it is not the whole story. Most boards are supplied with a set of instructions for rigging which you should read and follow. There is, however, a general procedure which applies to all but a few boards. The procedure is this:

Step 1: Bring the uphaul from below through the eye in the inner (foremost) boom end fitting and secure it with a figure-of-eight knot. Make further figure-of-eights in the uphaul spaced eight inches or so apart — but not too many, or the uphaul will end up too short. Before you tie the penultimate knot, pass the shock cord through the figure-of-eight and make it fast with a bowline. The other end of the cord can in due course be secured to the downhaul eye above the mast foot.

Step 2: Slide the mast into the sleeve on the sail.

Step 3: Insert the battens. They are much more difficult to slide in once the sail has been tensioned.

Step 4: Secure the inhaul to the mast through the cut-out section in the mast sleeve. First make a figure-of-eight, then a rolling hitch or cow hitch, but do not pull them tight just yet. (Most boards now have their own simple boom/mast attachment systems.)

Step 5: Secure the downhaul with a bowline and insert the mast foot. Double the downhaul and use a single

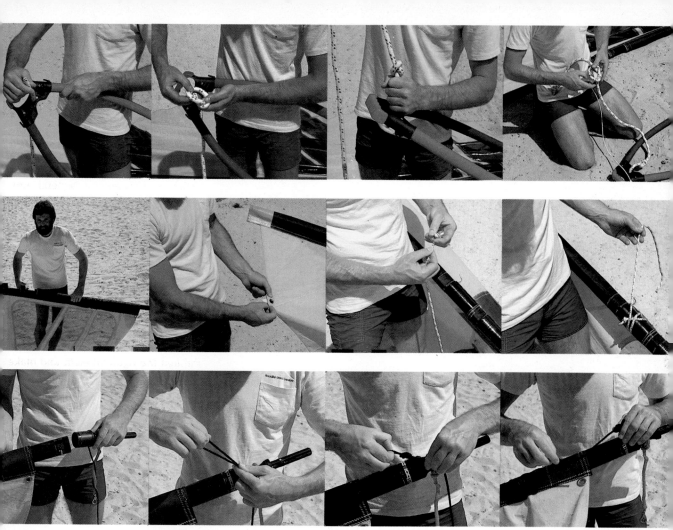

half-hitch to make a loop, then take the free end of the line, lead it through the cringle in the sail and back through the loop. Pull the downhaul taut and make it fast immediately below the cringle with two half-hitches.

Step 6: The rolling hitch or cow hitch securing the inhaul to the mast can now be correctly positioned and

drawn tight. The free end should be pulled directly forward. Position the inhaul so that once you are sailing the boom will be at shoulder or eye level when the mast is vertical.

Step 7: How you secure the boom will depend largely on the design of the inner boom end fitting. Most models have two eyes and a jam cleat. If the cleat is on the left, bring the inhaul down through the eye on the right, round the rear of the mast and then up through the other eye. If the cleat is on the right, start with the eye on the left. Now draw the inhaul taut and secure it to the cleat. This way you ensure that the boom is firmly held by the part of the inhaul that is led round the mast. Secure the free end behind the cleat with a half-hitch so that it cannot slip out.

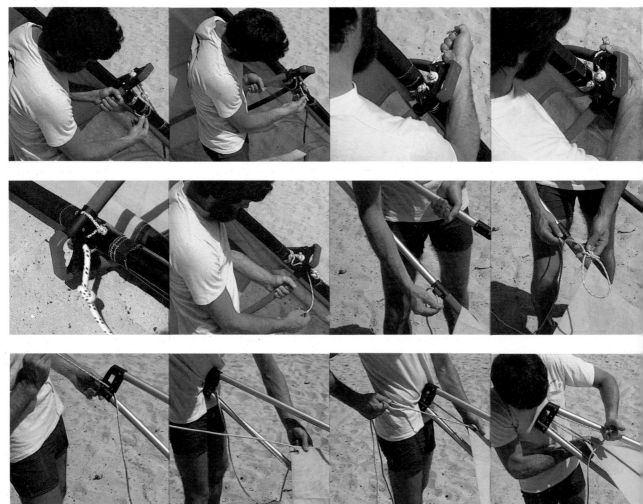

Step 8: The outhaul is now made fast to one of the two jam cleats positioned one on each side of the boom. To prevent it slipping out, put a figure-of-eight or bowline in the free end (a bowline provides you with a convenient loop to draw the outhaul tight with, should you need to). Now take the other end of the outhaul and lead it through one of the two eyes in the outer boom end fitting — the eye on the right if it is going to be made fast to the cleat on the right of the boom, and vice versa. From there, pass the end through the clew cringle and back through the other end in the boom end fitting. Finally haul the sail taut and make the outhaul fast on the second cleat without losing tension.

On some rigs with relatively inflexible masts tensioning the sail requires a lot of effort. Rest the boom end against your tummy and grasp the foot of the sail with your hand. Then pull the foot towards you while your other hand pulls the outhaul through the cleat.

The last job is to attach the little hook on the shock cord at the end of the uphaul to the mast foot. Your rig is now ready for the water.

Finally, a couple of words about sail tension. If a sail looks creased once rigged, something is wrong. The most common fault is incorrect tensioning of either downhaul or outhaul. First, draw the downhaul so tight that a large fold appears at the luff of the sail, parallel with the mast, and re-secure. Then retension the outhaul by pulling on it until the fold disappears and there are no more small folds or creases perpendicular to the boom.

Unrigging

A quick method of unrigging, when you don't want to dismantle the rig completely, is to do the following:

1. Release the outhaul.
2. Remove the battens.
3. Roll the sail up to the mast. The battens can be slipped into the rolls for safekeeping, but make sure they lie parallel to the mast.
4. Lay the boom against the mast.
5. Use the uphaul to secure the boom to the mast.

Learning to boardsail: Practice

First exercises with the rig

Strength is a relatively unimportant requirement in a boardsailor; far more vital are technique and a sense of balance. The first thing to learn is how to balance on the board, then how to control the sail. Finally, everything comes together when you learn to co-ordinate these two basic skills.

All this should present no problems if you start off by practising each new technique, beginning with raising sail and moving on to sailing round a circle, on the so-called 'dry land rig'. This is not a simulator, but simply your own mast, sail and boom without the board, and will give you the right feel for sail and wind. In addition, you won't keep falling into the water every time you make a mistake; you'll simply find yourself sitting on your bottom. Especially in stronger winds these dry-lands exercises can be quite fun, and they are very easy for beginners to get the hang of.

Lay your rig on the ground in such a way that the mast is pointing away from the wind. As you raise the sail it is best to step on the mast foot to discourage the rig from sliding away.

You can, of course, do the exercises on the beach with the board, although the fin should be removed first. Lay the board down so that it lies at right angles to the wind, and insert

The secret of boardsailing: you steer by inclining the whole rig.

the foot of the mast in its socket. In boardsailing schools dry-land exercises start with a simulator, which is a rig fitted on a board or simple platform mounted on a pivot so that it can turn through 360 degrees, sometimes on gimbals and braked by little hydraulic shock absorbers or springs. The pupil can then practise steering the board by inclining the rig, as the simulator will turn in the same way as a real board will on water. When you get to the section on raising sail, try all the exercises out on dry land first. It works wonders!

Balancing on the board

"But it's so wobbly!" Everyone begins their first lesson on the board with this observation, but it is not long before you develop a sense of balance and a feel for the board beneath your feet. Just take your board, with the centreboard but without the rig, and wade out into water no more than about hip-deep. Climb

on to the board from the side, somewhere near the centreboard.

Now stand up, using outstretched arms to maintain your balance. Move forward, towards the bow of the board, then back towards the stern. Try a jump turn: start with your feet facing the bow, jump up and twist through 90 degrees so that you land with your feet pointing towards the board rail. Then do the same with a half-turn. With a little imagination you can invent your own exercises; practise until you feel perfectly confident on the board.

The first beginner's exercise: standing and balancing on the board without the sail.

Carrying board and rig down to the water

You have now rigged your board, and checked out wind and weather. Before you go afloat, there are two golden rules you should learn:

● Always carry the rig and the board into to the water separately. A board with its rig in place is far too unwieldy to transport.
● Take the rig into the water first. The rig will remain where you put it, and won't start drifting away, because part of it is underwater and thus acts as a sort of sea anchor. The board, on the other hand, will drift away very rapidly or in heavy waves may be thrown ashore with sufficient force to damage the fin.

Over short distances you can carry the rig above your head, with the sail set up and properly tensioned. One hand holds the boom, the other the mast. The mast foot, or the mast itself, should face into the wind so that the wind helps to carry the sail as you walk down towards the shore.

If you are further from the water it is best to roll the sail up and fold the boom against the mast, and carry the package down to the shore before completing the rigging and throwing it into the water.

The easiest way to carry the rig is to hold it above your head and then throw it into the water.

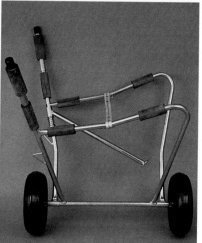

The best way to carry the board is to hold it underarm with your hand in the centreboard slot.

Trolleys such as these take the effort out of carrying your equipment to the water.

The board can be carried easily under one arm if you hold it by the centreboard slot with one hand and by the mast socket with the other. If you find this too unwieldy, insert the centreboard, which will give you another convenient handhold. If two of you are going sailing, of course, the easiest solution is to carry a board under each arm with one of you in front, one behind.

You can buy little trolleys if it is a long distance down to the water. Designed to take either the board or the whole set-up, these make transport considerably easier.

Paddling with the sail rigged

Dismantling the rig in the water

Before you go too far out from the shore it is essential that you know how to get back if the wind dies or becomes too strong for you. One effective method in the first instance is to lower the rig down on to the stern of the board (but don't remove the mast foot from its socket), so that the sail touches the water in as few places as possible. Then, either kneeling or lying on the bow of the board, paddle using your hands or the centreboard.

There is another method whereby you remove the mast foot from its socket and lay the rig down with the boom across the board and the masthead pointing forward. Then lie down on the board as shown in the photograph, with the boom below you and the sail balanced on your back and feet. Now paddle using your hands.

If the wind has freshened you may not be able to make any progress to windward without dismantling the rig. As it is quite difficult to do this out on the water, it is best to practise packing up the rig on land or at least in shallow water first.

1. Undo the mast leash and take the mast foot out of its socket on the board.
2. Release the clip on the shock cord from the downhaul.
3. Let go one side of the clew outhaul.
4. Take the foot of the sail and roll it up towards the mast. The battens can sometimes be left in the sail, but it is a sensible precaution against breakage to remove them and roll them within the sail.
5. Fold the boom up against the mast.
6. Use the uphaul and its shock cord to secure the foot of the rolled-up sail to the mast.
7. Secure the outer boom end and the masthead end of the sail to the mast with the outhaul.
8. Lay the rig on the board so that the mast foot points forward.

It is important that you roll the sail up *quickly* and *tightly*. Every square inch of packaged sail increases your windage and accentuates the leeway you make and every minute you lose carries you further away. No matter

In a calm the easiest way to get back ashore is to leave the sail rigged and lie underneath it. In a strong wind it is best to roll it up and lay it on the board or even use it as a paddle (right).

46

where you started off from, always paddle towards the nearest bit of land, where you will be able to find calmer water. Once near the beach you can turn and start paddling along the shore towards your base.

If you are a long way from home you can use the mast as a paddle.

This means fully dismantling the rig on the board, rolling the sail up as tightly as you can and sitting or kneeling while you paddle as if you were in a canoe.

This is only practical in light winds, as higher waves will make it impossible to paddle, and as dismantling the rig will cost valuable time, during which you will be drive further downwind. And remember: if need be, jettison the rig completely — better claim on the insurance for a new one, than risk drowning but *never, ever* leave your board — it is your liferaft until help arrives.

Raising sail

When raising sail the feet should be positioned either side of the mast foot. With the uphaul in one hand you can balance quite easily.

After all these exercises, you're now ready to learn how to boardsail. It's a warm summer day, and you watch with envy another sailor gliding effortlessly over the water. Suppress your envy: in a couple of hours you will be doing the same.

The first thing to learn is how to raise the sail from the water with the minimum of effort. Lay the rig in the water so that the masthead points directly downwind. The board should be at right angles to the mast and to windward of it. Fit the mast foot into its socket.

Now climb onto the board from the windward side. Grasp the lowest knot in the uphaul with your arm outstretched, and with a straight back, position yourself with your back to the wind and your feet a hand's breadth either side of the mast foot. This is the basic stance for raising sail.

Now, with arms and back straight and legs slightly bent, lean backwards so that the masthead lifts from the water. Wait until the sail has drained itself of water and the resistance has reduced, then work your way hand over hand and knot by knot along the uphaul so that the sail slowly but smoothly comes up.

Take care that you don't haul the sail up too quickly, or the sudden lack

Lift the rig gently and smoothly, then...

of resistance will cause you to over-balance and topple backwards into the water.

Now grasp the mast with one or both hands at a point just below the boom. Hold it almost vertical, with arms outstretched. The boom outer end will come out of the water and the sail will start to slat in the wind. Your knees should be slightly bent, your trunk upright, your head up. The sail will now be at right angles to the board with the clew pointing directly downwind and also indicating the wind direction.

You should avoid bending over forwards as you raise sail, this overloads the spinal column and wastes a lot of energy. Take care to raise the sail directly over the mast foot, or the board will respond by turning in line with the boom. If the rig slips to one side while you are raising sail, pull it in the opposite direction so that it comes back to the correct angle.

. . . as soon as the outer boom end leaves the water, the sail will start to slat in the wind and the pressure will ease.

Raising sail to windward

Normally the sail will be lying to lee-ward when you lift it. But after a fall to windward or if board and rig are left to their own devices for some time, you will find the rig following you into the water on the wrong side to windward. With the wind pressure acting on it, raising sail again will be rather difficult. The following tech-nique will allow you to bring the rig back easily on to the leeward side of the board where it belongs. Stand on the board, feet either side of the mast foot, facing to windward, towards the sail. Use the uphaul to pull the rig halfway out of the water, or less in stronger winds. The wind will get under the sail and push it to one side. Keep the mast at right angles to the board so that board and rig are pulled round slowly to face in the right direc-tion, after which you can simply raise sail as usual. Needless to say this is a rather more strenuous exercise then simply raising sail to windward.

Another faster and more elegant method is to lift the rig halfway out of the water again, and hold the board in position with your feet so that it doesn't turn; then lift the rig to the point at which only the outer boom end is still in the water. The wind will catch the sail and push it towards you. Now give a little jerk to free the rig fully from the water, and it will flick over the board to leeward. You will have to be pretty nimble on your feet, switching position to get round the other side of the mast foot and hold the sail to prevent it falling in the water again on the leeward side.

This technique is less of a time-waster, and as the board is prevented from turning during the manoeuvre — which is not the case with the pre-vious method — you end up still facing in the right direction. But it is more difficult, and requires practice and a good sense of balance.

If the rig is lying to windward, the moment it is raised from the water it will snap over to the other side of the board.

Turning

Before you set off — however eager you may be — you must be able to turn your board where you will. Turning is without doubt the single most important technique in board-sailing; even before you learn to go about and gybe, you will need to know how to turn to avoid obstacles and, of course, to get home again.

Remember raising sail? If the mast was not raised directly in line with its socket, or step, the board began to turn of its own accord. When in the basic mast abeam position, if the rig is not balanced directly over the mast foot, the same thing will happen. The effect you were trying to avoid while raising sail, because it caused the board to twist round, becomes the principle that allows you to turn when you want to.

Stand in the basic mast abeam posi-tion as before with your feet either side of the mast foot, hold the mast with one or both hands and let the sail flap with the outer boom end just out of the water.

If you now lean the rig towards the stern, the sail will begin to fill with wind. The board will start to move and the bow will turn towards the wind. If you lean the rig towards the bow, the bow will turn to leeward away from the wind, the stern into wind. At the same time, shuffle round the mast so that you keep your back to the wind until the board is pointing in the required direction.

While this is going on, the sail will keep the same orientation, pointing downwind. Your position does not change either; you stay with your back to the wind. Only the board will

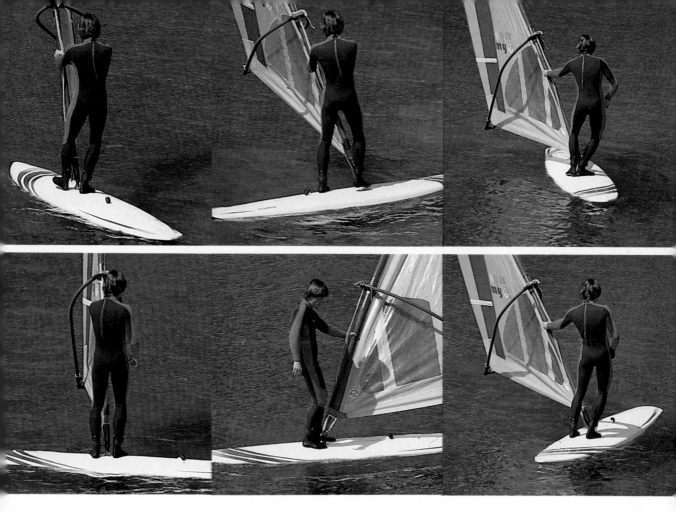

turn, and it will continue to do so while the mast is raked and while you help it round with your feet.

Thus:

If you lean the mast towards the bow —

The board will turn to leeward, away from the wind.

If you lean the mast towards the stern —

The board will turn to windward, towards the wind.

You should now be able to turn your board so that it is facing in the opposite direction — to make a half-turn. A 360-degree turn means causing the board to revolve through a full circle, while you and the sail continue to face in the same direction as before. Practise both manoeuvres in bigger waves and a fresher wind as well, which will boost your confidence and improve your sense of balance.

The board is turned by inclining the mast towards the bow or the stern. If at the same time you slowly work your way round the mast, you can make the board rotate through a full circle.

Getting under way

The basic start: face the rig, then tilt it to windward past your upper body, while twisting your head and shoulders to face in the direction of travel. Only then, grasp the boom with the sheet hand and pull (sheet in).

Many beginners make the mistake of thinking that, having bought a sailboard, they can simply head for the nearest stretch of water and get sailing. But anything more than a light breeze will quickly show the advantage of some dry-land training. Novices who have spent just a short time on a simulator will have learnt to balance and turn, and will have already developed a feel for board and rig before stepping out into the water. It is all a matter of getting the right technique.

Practise the start on land first, with just the rig, or on a simulator. After this 'dry run' the first time afloat will go a lot easier, and you will take much less time to become proficient.

Let's begin. You start with the same mast abeam position as before: that is to say, with the board perpendicular to the wind, the mast at right angles to the board and pointing directly downwind. Stand with your back to the wind, feet a hand's breadth either side of the foot of the mast. Grasp the mast just under the boom end with the hand nearest the bow — if the bow is to your right, the right hand, and vice versa. This is your mast hand.

Now move the foot nearest the stern to one side as far as the centreboard slot, and the other foot to the back of the mast. Pull the rig gently to windward past your body until the boom is parallel with the water. The rig must be pulled far enough windward that it feels quite light and will momentarily stay balanced if you let go.

The sheet hand (the hand nearest the stern) is for the moment free. As you tilt the rig let your trunk twist round so that it is at right angles to the board and you can see ahead through the window in the sail. Now grasp the boom with your sheet hand a good shoulder's breadth away from the mast, then move your mast hand from the mast to the forward end of the boom. Your elbows should not be tensed, but hang loosely down.

At the moment there is no pressure on the sail, which is flapping free. Use your sheet hand to pull the boom gradually towards you which will cause your trunk to turn back again.

Transfer your weight to your back foot and look in the direction of travel. You are now in the sailing position.

Getting under way — a resumé
● Mast hand grasps mast
● Rearmost foot moves to centreboard slot
● Foremost foot just behind mast
● The mast hand pulls the rig to windward (Important: tilt the mast far enough to windward so that the boom is parallel with the water and you can see through the window)
● At the same time, let your trunk twist round to face towards the front of the board
● Sheet hand grasps the boom
● Mast hand grasps the boom
● Sheet hand pulls in gently, as you turn back once more to face the sail.

If you let your trunk twist back again, so that your sheet hand lets the boom out a bit, the sail will lose pressure and the board will slow or stop. Your hands should always remain the same distance apart, with your shoulders kept parallel to the boom.

Twisting your trunk towards the wind and simultaneously pulling with the sheet hand until the outer boom end is almost above the leeward side of the board is known as 'sheeting in'. The opposite, when you let the boom out and turn away from the wind, is called 'easing'.

Before every start you must of course ensure that you have clear water ahead of you and are not likely to impede or endanger anyone.

The most common, practically universal mistake among beginners is a failure to rake the mast far enough to

Falls are a necessary part of learning

windward. If you don't, when you sheet in the rig will be pulled aft, the board will turn into wind and you will fall in. So the golden rule is:
Mast to windward

Sailing straight

Now the real fun of boardsailing is getting closer. Maintaining an equilibrium between board and rig, the increasing speed gives you your first real taste of sailing.

You have to watch the rig the whole time to make sure it is at the correct rake and sheeted in to the required point.

You need the correct rake to steer the board and maintain directional stability, as we discovered when practising how to turn. You should also watch out that the board doesn't turn bow into wind (called 'luffing') or away from the wind (called 'bearing away'). You therefore have to keep adjusting the rake of the rig in order to keep the board sailing straight.

Remember:

Mast raked forward: bow turns away from wind — board bears away
Mast raked aft: bow turns toward the wind — board luffs up

You also have to control the sail setting, especially in a gusty wind. The sail should be sheeted in to the point at which it just stops flapping. If you can ease the sail by letting out your sheet hand and twisting your trunk towards the bow, the sail is sheeted in too hard. Sheet in only as far as is necessary to stop the sail flapping.

The rake is controlled with the mast hand, the trim of the sail with the sheet hand.

This is the right position to adopt in boardsailing: arms straight, the body leaning straight back into wind.

Wrong: if your forward foot is in front of the mast, the board will bury its nose in the water.

In light airs you will be able to stand upright. Keep your knees slightly bent, so that you can absorb the movement of the board over small waves or choppy water. The forward foot is used to transfer the pressure on the sail, which is transmitted from boom through the arms to the body, to the board.

In fresher wind you will have to hang to windward from the boom. Keep your body straight, and don't adopt the classic boomerang attitude of most novices. Bottom in, shoulders out is the rule. Be brave, and hang from the boom so that the wind pressure on the sail is supporting you. Naturally it will take a while before you master this technique on the water.

Once you have mastered the technique and can feel how the board can be steered with both feet, and can hang out casually over the water as you glide along, the fascination of boardsailing will be starting to get to you. The nearness of the water and

the direct interplay between you and the wind and the waves are the things that thrill so many boardsailors.

It can happen that your board buries its nose in the water when sailing straight. This can be remedied by bringing both feet back towards the stern a little so that your weight is concentrated further aft. Sailing straight ahead for even a short distance gives you a great sense of achievement.

At the beginning your arms, unused to the stress, will ache. To relieve this there are a couple of alternative ways of gripping the boom:

● The wrist grip — the conventional one in normal conditions
● The under-grip — used mostly by the mast hand, which is more comfortable ergonomically
● The elbow — grip which offloads the underarm
● The shoulder grip — especially energy-saving, when beating in stronger winds.

Luffing up and bearing away

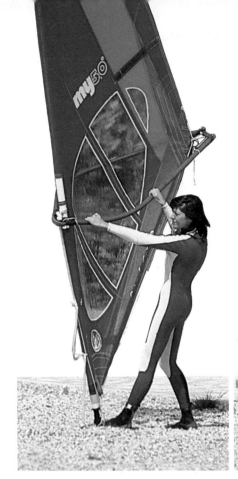

In boardsailing there are two basic methods of altering direction:

● Luffing up, when the bow turns toward the wind
● Bearing away, when the bow turns away from the wind

As you have already learnt, you can steer your board by raking the mast forward or aft. Remember the exercise:

If you rake the mast aft, the board luffs up — turns towards the wind
If you rake the mast forward, the board bears away — turns away from the wind.

This is why a sailboard does not need the rudder required to steer a dinghy, and is a function of the relationship between centre of effort and centre of lateral resistance. Later on, in the section on the theory of sailing you will find an answer to the question of why and how. In practice what happens is this:

Luffing up

You are sailing straight, with the wind blowing at right angles to the board. This is the point of sailing known as reaching. If you want to luff up, incline the mast towards the stern. Switch your weight on to your aft foot in order to push the board into the turn. Throughout the manoeuvre the rig should be upright when viewed from ahead. Sheet in the sail, which should remain full all the time and

not be allowed to start flapping.

Your board has now come up towards the wind, that is to say you are no longer reaching but 'close-hauled'. If you luff up yet further, leaving the mast raked aft, the board will continue to turn until it is facing directly head to wind. The wind will be blowing on to the bow, and your board will stop with the sail flapping, as it is impossible to sail directly into

Bearing away

Again start on a reach, sailing parallel to the waves and with the wind on the beam. To bear away, rake the mast sharply forwards towards the bow, shift your weight onto your front foot and force the bow of the board round into the turn.

As you bear away the angle at which the wind hits the board will change, so you will have to ease the sail out with your sheet hand until it just stops lifting at the luff. With the wind blowing over the quarter you will be sailing on a broad reach.

If you carry on bearing away so that the wind comes from directly behind you will move from a broad reach to a run, following the same downwind course as the waves. For this you must stand exactly in the middle of the board, with the centreboard slot between your feet. The sail should be eased until it is at right angles to the board and you can see ahead through the window.

When you bear away on to a broad reach the speed of the board increases very rapidly. Wind pressure on the sail increases, and you will have to be ready for it. Brace yourself

firmly on the board with your front foot and lean backwards. If you don't, in stronger winds the sail will simply pull you over the bow into the water in what is graphically termed a catapult fall.

To recap:
To bear away rake the mast forward along the plane of the sail, and ease the sail until the luff just stops lifting. Brace yourself against the board with your front foot, and lean backwards.

Practise luffing up and bearing away by following a snaky course. Get under way on a beam reach, then luff up and sail close-hauled for a bit. Bear away on to a beam reach again, then on to a broad reach. Try this exercise several times until you have fixed firmly in your mind the two basic rules which follow and until you can carry out the manoeuvres automatically and without thinking. You will be surprised how accurately you can steer your board — to within a few degrees.

To luff up: incline the mast towards the stern in the plane of the sail
To bear away: incline the mast towards the bow in the plane of the sail

wind. You should therefore only rake the mast for a short while, deliberately and smoothly. After the manoeuvre the mast should be firmly raked forward, a little less than when you were reaching, as you are now sailing at a more acute angle to the wind than before. So: To luff up rake the mast aft, sheet in the sail and transfer your weight to your back foot.

The points of sailing

A sailor describes the course he is following by reference to the direction of the wind rather than some point on the land. He therefore has to know where the wind is coming from at any moment. It is impossible to sail directly into wind; if you turn head to wind the sail will simply flog without giving any drive.

Close-hauled

Also known as beating into the wind, this is the course you follow when the wind is blowing at some 45 degrees from dead ahead. Wind pressure on the sail is here at its greatest, and you can only travel forwards because of the action of the centreboard, which limits the drift to leeward. The sail should be hauled in as tight as possible. It is the slowest point of sailing.

Tacking

Although you cannot sail head to wind, the fact that you can sail at 45 degrees either to right or to left of windward makes it possible to reach a point directly upwind by a zigzag series of close-hauled legs, first to one side, then to the other. This is known as tacking.

When doing this it is important to make all the progress you can to windward so that you can reach your destination in fewer tacks. You should therefore sail as close to the wind as possible, and avoid any tendency to bear away onto a reach.

Reaching

With the wind coming over the beam, in other words at right angles to the fore-and-aft line of the board, you are on a beam reach. The board will be sailing significantly faster than when close-hauled, parallel to the waves. The sail should be eased out, and the centreboard half raised as the tendency to drift to leeward will be much less marked.

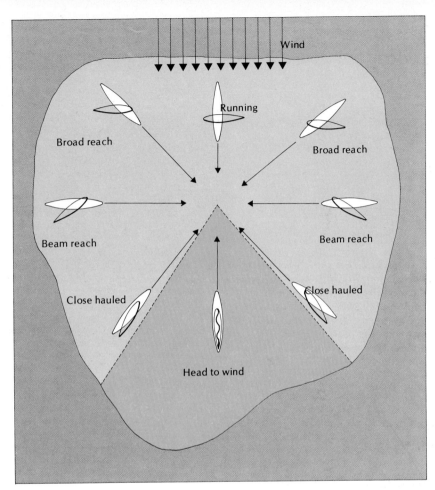

Diagram labels: Wind, Running, Broad reach, Broad reach, Beam reach, Beam reach, Close hauled, Close hauled, Head to wind

Broad reaching

When you bear away from a beam reach, the wind moves round to blow from the quarter. You are now broad reaching, which is the fastest point of sailing. The sail is eased out; the centreboard can be almost fully raised as the board is virtually sailing before the wind and is subject to very little leeway.

Running

If you bear away from a broad reach until the wind blows from dead astern you come on to a run. You will now be sailing with the wind and sea at your back. Position yourself in the middle of the board, with the centreboard between your feet and the sail eased out so that it is at right angles to the board and you can see ahead through the window.

This point of sailing tends to be uncomfortable, as you can only shift your weight across the beam and no longer fore and aft to keep your balance. But lots of practice and a sense of balance should enable you to overcome these difficulties.

Steering on this course is simple. Incline the rig to the right, and the board will turn to the left; incline it to the left, the board will turn to the right. The centreboard is now redundant, as you are now sailing downwind, in the same direction as any leeway; the centreboard would act merely as a brake, and should be fully raised.

Manoeuvring

You are now more confident and balanced and competent enough to use luffing up and bearing away. By dropping and re-raising the sail you can even get back to the point you started from.

But the method of turning we have hitherto discussed is ungainly and time-consuming, as you have to stop the board every time you wish to change direction, and then start off again. Especially when tacking, you need all the windward progress, you can get, and this laborious method is uneconomical and impractical.

You will by now realise that when you turn the board round and sail off in the other direction, the sail will change sides. The sailor talks of sailing on the port or starboard tack. If the wind is coming from anywhere on the port side (the left side of the board when looking forward), he is on port tack; with the wind coming over the starboard or right-hand side, he is on starboard tack.

Starboard = right
Port = left
when viewed from the stern looking forward

Going about, or tacking

We are now going to cover a method of changing direction whereby you shunt the sail to the other side of the board and set off on another tack without losing momentum and halting the board. This is called 'going about', or tacking; starting off close-hauled on one tack, you luff up into the wind, turn the bow past the wind direction and bear away onto a close-hauled course on the opposite tack.

The procedure is as follows. Sailing close-hauled and straight, glance forward into the wind to check that the way is clear. Grasp the mast just below

the boom with your mast hand, without altering the trim of the sail. Place your forward foot in front of the mast, and luff up by tilting the mast backwards until the board is head to wind. Now let go of the boom with your sheet hand, step round to the front of the mast so that you are facing astern and so that the outer end of the boom is hanging over the stern.

From here on your hands trade jobs; what was your sheet hand becomes your mast hand, while the former mast hand becomes the sheet hand. Grasp the mast with the former sheet hand.

Step round to the other side of the mast. Take up the same position as you adopted to get under way the first time, and that's it. You have gone about.

As the board turns through the wind

you lose your drive (since there is no more wind pressure on the sail) and with it your means of support. This can be overcome by performing the manoeuvre rapidly; the faster you change sides, the sooner you will have pressure on the sail again and be able to support yourself with the rig. You should therefore tack with as great a swing as possible; this calls for vigorous luffing and bearing away, so that you luff up and bear away as smoothly and quickly as possible without getting caught 'in irons', head to wind with the sail flapping.

The luffing up that precedes a tack should be emphatic, not to say exaggerated. Incline the mast towards the stern so far that the boom almost touches the water. If you now haul in the sail with your sheet hand until the boom is poised virtually over the centre of the board, you will have enough swing to take you through the wind.

Bearing away should be as overstated as was luffing up. Rake the mast well forward until the bow of the board is pointing in the direction in which you wish to travel, then bring it back into the normal position for sailing straight. Every time you tack the mast and sheet hands will swap roles.

The more you practise on the water, the faster and more expert you will become at this manoeuvre until you hardly have to think about it at all.

Gybing

The gybe is one of the most enjoyable basic skills in boardsailing. It introduces you for the first time to the amazing manoeuvrability of your board; once you know how, gybing is much easier than going about, and a lot more fun, as it can be executed faster and more fluently. All you need is a good sense of balance and good co-ordination.

You start the gybe by bearing away onto a broad reach and then a run, but instead of straightening up onto the run you continue the turn so that the back of the board swings through the wind and the sail swings round the bow to fill on the opposite side.

Let's go through that step by step. Check that you have clear water to leeward, then bear away onto a run.

Now move your forward foot towards the stern, and the rear foot up to meet it. Grasp the mast with your mast hand, letting go of the boom with your sheet hand. The sail will swing over the bow, that is gybe. Mast and sheet hand now change over, just as in the tack.

In contrast to the tack, where you have to shuffle round in front of the mast to get to the other side, the gybe requires you to stay in the same position directly over the centreboard slot. If you are broad reaching, a gybe will effect a 90-degree change of course. On a run, however, there will only be a very small change of course. With the wind blowing from dead astern it makes little difference which side the sail is being carried, as the rig will lie straight across the beam of the board, with the mast either to port or to starboard. Nevertheless, sailors still talk of being on 'starboard tack' or 'port tack'.

When running before the wind:

If the mast is to port, you are on the port tack.
If the mast is to starboard, you are on the starboard tack.

If you luff up too sharply after the gybe and come onto a broad reach or even a beam reach, the board will pick up speed very rapidly, especially in stronger winds. If you are not ready for the sudden increase in pressure on the sail, you might find yourself dragged forward to make a spectacular catapult fall.

If you prepare yourself for the tug from the sail, and stand with your feet firmly planted and your trunk inclined backwards, you will only need a little practice to master the gybe.

When tacking the bow turns through the wind, while the sail swings over the stern.
When gybing the stern turns through the wind, while the sail swings over the bow.

Sailing in a circle

Learning to sail the board in a circle is a valuable exercise that enables you to consolidate most of the techniques we have introduced so far.

Try to sail round a buoy. If you have mastered the tack and the gybe, this should present no problem. Initially the circle you describe will be quite wide, but you should try to make it progressively smaller and faster, first in light breezes and then in stronger winds.

The exercise consists of luffing up, going about, bearing away on to a run, gybing and then luffing up until you are once again pointing in the original direction.

Once you have mastered sailign in a circle you will be ready to learn some more advanced techniques.

Falling in

Even after you have mastered all the techniques described so far and can sail the board competently in all directions, you may find yourself falling in. The fall is an integral part of boardsailing. Don't worry about the laughter from on shore that will accompany your involuntary swims when you first start learning. Everyone began the same way, and falling in is the order of the day even for expert boardsailors.

But one thing you should learn is how to fall. As with judo, it is important to fall correctly so that you do not injure yourself or damage your board.

You should always try to fall on the opposite side of the board to the rig. If you see a fall coming, try to push the sail to leeward. If you can't, and you fall in to windward with the sail on top of you, stick your arms up and push yourself towards the luff or leech. From there you will be able to climb back on board.

You need not be concerned while under the sail. Between the water and the sail there is always a large pocket of air. You will find yourself automatically raising a hand above your head to fend off the sail as it drops.

The most important rule when falling in is: *don't panic!* This simply uses up energy that you will need underwater. Don't tense up: allow your muscles to relax as you fall, then, once you have surfaced and got your bearings and your breath back, climb back on the board again. Remember, if you don't fall in, you will never be a good boardsailor.

After you have climbed back on board, rest for a minute or two before setting off again, so that you relax and give your muscles a chance to recover their strength.

After a fall, leave the rig where it is and rest for a while — you'll be in good company more often than not.

Loosening-up exercises

After your first few times out on the board you will arrive home with fierce aches in your muscles. Most of this is due not so much to effort as to the tensions that your inexperience will build up. Once you know how to sail straight, your forearms will begin to ache. It is important that you take a rest now and then to give your muscles a chance to recover and to release the tension in your body.

Sit on the board, with the rig lying in the water, and move your arms about. Hold them up in the air, so that you can get the blood flowing again. The more frequently you go boardsailing, the less necessary these loosening-up exercises will become, as your forearm and finger muscles get used to the load.

You can also try a few exercises at home to build up your muscles:
1. Hook your fingers together and pull hard. Then do the same with your thumbs.
2. Squeeze a soft tennis ball in each hand.
3. Clasp your left wrist with your right hand, and try to bend the left arm while at the same time resisting the pressure with your right. Then try the same exercise with the right wrist and left hand.

Learning to sail: Theory

The aerodynamic principles of sailing

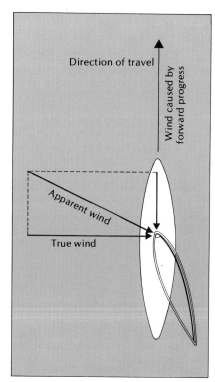

Direction of travel

Wind caused by forward progress

Apparent wind

True wind

The board is driven along by the apparent wind, which is a combination of true wind and the wind caused by the board's forward progress.

How is it that a sailboard can be driven forward by a wind that is blowing from the beam or even from ahead of the beam? It sounds impossible — but it's not.

The wind that you feel as you stand on the bank we call the true wind. there are two other winds that are important to the sailor. Imagine that you are on a bicycle on a totally windless day. Despite the lack of wind you can feel a breeze from directly ahead, caused by and equal to the speed of your bicycle. A sailboard moving through the action of the true wind will also meet wind generated by its forward motion.

The boardsailor, of course, cannot distinguish between the two winds acting upon his board. Instead, he feels what is called the apparent wind, blowing from a direction somewhere between the true wind and the wind that it generates by its forward motion. This is the wind that acts on the sail, not the true wind. The direction of the true wind is only discernible by reference to something fixed on land, such as a flag, chimney smoke or the sail of a beached dinghy.

Important: you are driven along by the apparent wind.

If you are on a dead run, some of the true wind blowing directly over the stern of the board will be cancelled out by the wind from ahead caused by your motion through the water.

If you are sailing on a beam reach, with the true wind blowing at 90 degrees ot the fore-and-aft line of the board, the relative wind will lie somewhere between the beam and the bow. This can best be illustrated by the example of a steamship. In a beam wind the plume of of smoke from its funnel will not steam out directly abeam, but will be carried aft by the wind of the ship's forward movement; the faster the ship is travelling, the further aft streams the smoke.

The same principle applies to board-sailing. The faster you are sailing, the further forward the apparent wind moves, and the harder the sail has to be sheeted in. The sail of a slow, heavy displacement yacht on a beam reach might therefore be carried quite far out, whereas the sail of a fast cata-maran going in exactly the same direction would have to be sheeted in hard.

In a gust you can usually luff up, because the true wind increases rela-tive to the wind of the board's pro-gress, and brings the apparent wind aft.

It is easy to understand how the power of the wind is converted to for-ward movement on a run. The wind blows the sail along in front of it like a leaf; as it hits the rig it creates pressure on the sail and drives the board for-ward.

With the true wind blowing from the beam or ahead of the beam, however,

another principle comes into play, with the sail acting as a form of aerofoil. The airflow is diverted around the leading edge of the mast and along either side of the sail before converging again at the leech. On the windward side, there is high pressure and the airflow forces the sail into a curve. The air that passes along the other side of the sail, the leeward side, has further to go before it reaches the leech, and therefore has to travel faster. This causes a drop in pressure, a section, on the leeward side of the sail.

Pressure differences always try to even themselves out. As the fabric of the sail is impermeable, the only way of doing this is for the sail to give in to the relatively greater pressure on the windward side and allow itself to be sucked to leeward by the negative pressure zone there. This suction, which acts in a direction perpendicu-lar to the line of the boom, is the source of the sail's power.

The fact that the board does directly follow that direction is due to its underwater shape; the flat, surfaces of fin and centreboard convert the side-ways pressure into forward motion through the water.

Thus a sailing boat on a run is being pushed along by the wind, but on all other points of sailing, with the wind to one side, it owes its drive to a combina-tion of push and pull. As the pull of the aerofoil effect is greater than the push of the wind, the sail is drawn to wind-ward and takes both board and sailor with it.

The important components are therefore the aerofoil curve of the sail and the centreboard, which prevents the board from making too much lee-way. But the wind pressure is not con-verted fully into forward motion. When sailing upwind the force to pro-duce forward motion is at its least, and the closer you point towards the wind

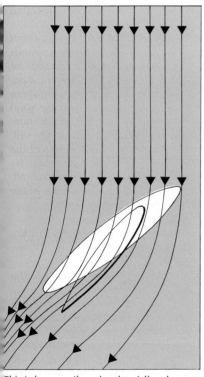

This is how a sail works: the airflow has to travel further on the lee side of the sail. This creates a negative pressure, a suction effect, which accounts for about two thirds of the sail's driving power.

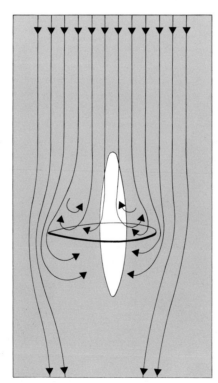

Sailing on a run is not so fast, as the shape of the sail simply 'catches' the wind, creating positive pressure on the windward side, but none of the 'extra' suction to leeward.

the weaker the drive becomes. Although the sail will remain full, it no longer pulls you ahead as effectively, something that you will notice in particular when tacking up a narrow channel. Bear away a little to get a good compromise between speed and closeness to the wind.

The forward producing forces are greatest on a beam reach. Here leeway force is significantly less than total driving force, so that more can go into driving the board. Leeway is also much reduced.

Sail profile

You may from time to time hear board-sailors talking about the cut and set of their sails. A good 'cut' indicates that the 'motor' of your board will run smoothly, like a well-tuned car engine. The ideal sail should form a smooth aerofoil curve, with no ridges so that its wind resistance is as low as possible and so that the required suction can be built up on the leeward side.

The shape of the curve in the sail is known as camber or draft. A highly curved, full sail produces more power than a flat sail. The ratio of the depth of the curve to chord length (the horizontal distance between mast and clew) can vary in the case of a sailboard from about 5 per cent for very flat storm sails to 17 per cent for full, light-air sails. As a comparison, the spinnaker of a modern sailing boat will have a ratio of about 22 per cent.

A full sail cannot be sheeted hard in for close-hauled work without the luff lifting. The flatter a sail is, the less effort is needed to control it in any particular conditions. But a full sail will generate significantly more power in the same wind, as the pressure on the weather side and the suction on the leeward side increase. The deepest part of the camber can usually be found just in front of the middle of the sail, where the pressure difference is at its greatest. So the higher you sail the stronger the wind, the flatter that part

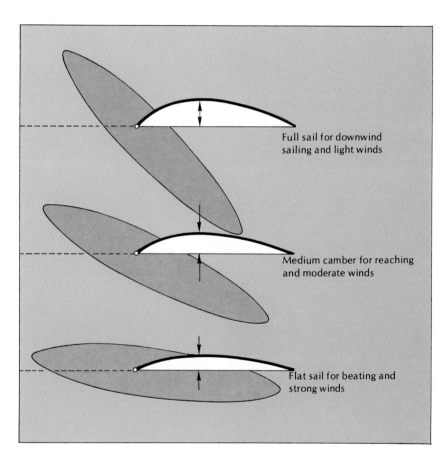

Full sail for downwind sailing and light winds

Medium camber for reaching and moderate winds

Flat sail for beating and strong winds

of the sail should be. Whereas it should be fuller when the wind is light and when sailing with the wind free. Sailing before the wind the sail should be quite full. Adjusting the fullness of the sail is known as tuning. It takes a lot of experience to learn to tune sails for optimum efficiency.

Steering

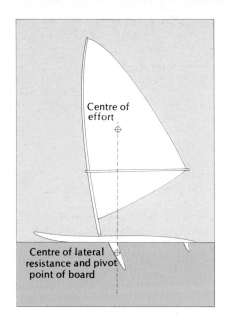

If the centre of effort on the sail lies directly over the centre of lateral resistance (effectively, the centre of gravity of the centreboard), the sailboard will travel in a straight line.

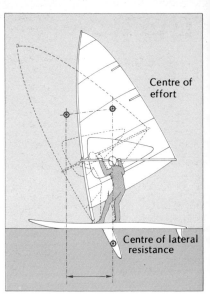

If you rake the rig forward, the centre of effort moves forward as well. It is now well ahead of the centre of lateral resistance, and the wind pushes the head of the board round, so that the board bears away.

Although the sailboard, unlike the sailing dinghy, has no rudder, it is possible to steer it to an accuracy of a few inches. How is this?

There is an imaginary point on the sail, known as the centre of effort, through which the total force of the wind can be said to act. The force is then transmitted by the mast foot, your own arms, body and feet to the board. The board in turn has its own point through which underwater forces can be said to act. This is termed the centre of lateral resistance, and is to be found more or less at the centre of gravity of the centreboard. If the centre of effort is directly above the centre of lateral resistance, the board will be balanced and sail straight ahead.

This is the case when the rig is slightly raked forward. If you rake it further forward, the centre of effort moves forward. The wind is now acting through a point that is well ahead of the centre of lateral resistance, and therefore pushes the bow away to leeward, so the board starts to bear away.

Precisely the opposite happens when you rake the mast aft. The centre of effort moves aft, the wind pushes the stern away from it, and you begin to turn to windward, or luff up.

So this is the fundamental difference between a sailing boat and a sailboard: as the boat has a fixed mast,

the centre of effort remains in the same position, so you need a rudder to alter course.

The mast on a sailboard, however, because of its universal joint can replace the rudder. If the sailor wants to bear away, he simply rakes the mast forward. This brings the centre of effort ahead of the centre of lateral resistance. If he wants to luff up he rakes the mast aft.

This principle of steering, in other words the shifting of the centre of effort, must become fixed firmly in your mind. It is the only way to develop automatic reactions whatever the weather and whatever board and sail you are using. From the very start your fundamental approach will be

better, especially in strong winds, gusty weather and surf.

If you want a flatter sail for close-hauled work or in strong winds, tighten up the downhaul and the outhaul. This will increase the curvature of the mast and the luff, and in so doing reduce the camber in the sail.

Uphaul and outhaul tight = flat sail for strong winds
Uphaul and outhaul slack = full sail for light winds

You should always adjust both uphaul and downhaul; never just one of them, or the sail will stretch and develop permanent ridges.

The Rule of the Road

Some popular stretches of water can get as crowded as a city street in rush hour. There will be scores of craft of all sorts afloat — sailboards, sportsboats, sailing dinghies, inflatables, rowing boats, fishing boats — as well as swimmers, skiers and divers. And every one of them needs some room.

As on the roads, anyone who doesn't know the rules is liable to get shouted at. And accidents caused by ignorance bring in their train prohibitions and restrictions.

But whereas on the roads you have a multitude of traffic signs to inform and give you instructions, water travel is not so restricted. Most of the laws that exist — known as the Collision Regulations — are designed to cater for vessels with poor manoeuvrability and relatively long stopping distances. Nevertheless there are basic rules that must be complied with even by boardsailors:

All vessels must be conducted in such a way that they do not endanger, damage or, except in unavoidable circumstances, inconvenience or obstruct another vessel.

Sailing boats and sailboards are treated alike by the Collision Regulations, as they both rely on the wind for their power. There are three rules that apply to two sailing craft approaching one another.

If you don't know the Collision Regulations, accidents will happen.

A typical boardsailing confrontation —
yellow and red sail should have kept clear.

1. Port gives way to starboard
If the wind is coming over the port side of your board, you are said to be sailing on the port tack, and vice versa. A boat on the port tack has to give priority to, or keep out of the way of, a boat on the starboard tack.

2. Windward gives way to leeward
When two craft are sailing on the same tack, the one that is furthest upwind has to keep out of the way of the other. You should always keep an eye on the water to leeward of you, either through the window or round the sail, as all vessels downwind of you and on the same tack will expect you to keep out of their way.

3. Overtaking craft keeps clear
If you want to overtake another board or a sailing boat you may, provided that you stay far enough clear to ensure that you do not disturb or endanger another craft. For the board-sailor this means at least two mast lengths, or at least ten metres, away. Which side you overtake on is up to you.

What happens when you meet a motor boat, a rowing boat or a commercial craft?

1. Power gives way to sail
In general, motor boats are expected to allow sailing craft right of way. A powered boat is, especially in lighter winds, much more manoeuvrable and often faster than a boat that relies on the wind for its speed. But don't deliberately cut someone up, just so that he has to get out of the way you could come off worst.

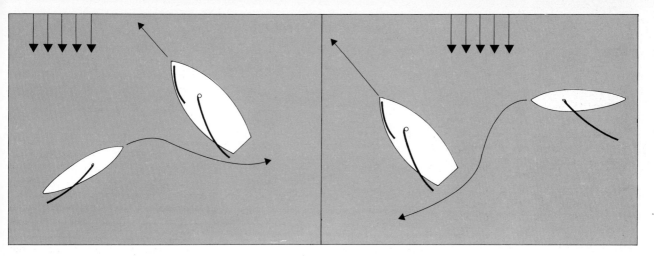

Port tack gives way to starboard.

Windward makes way for leeward.

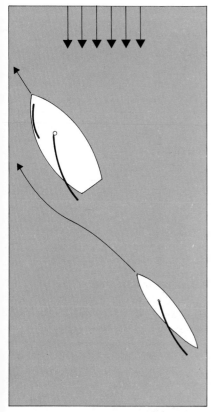

Overtaking boat keeps clear.

2. Rowing boats give way to sail

The rule that muscle-powered craft such as rowing boats, canoes and inflatables must give way to sailing craft is hardly practical. How can a small rubber dinghy be expected to get out of the way of a sailboard tearing down on it? You should also remember that owners of elementary craft such as these cannot necessarily be expected to know the rule of the road. Don't demand your right of way; it's best to give all muscle-powered craft a wide berth.

3. Beware big ships

Although you technically have right of way over all powered craft this does not give you the right in a narrow channel, to hamper the passage of a vessel that can only navigate inside such a channel. In practice this means that you should steer well clear of all commercial craft, from fishing boats and ferries to supertankers.

Swimmers at all times have right of way over any craft, whether under power or under sail. If there is a special strip of beach for the use of board-sailors, use it, and stay well clear of any bathers. You might find they approach you out of curiosity; but they are difficult to spot, especially in waves, with just a head visible above the surface. That head is particularly vulnerable; you can imagine the consequences if your sailboard were to run over it at full tilt.

A word of caution: never insist on your right of way to the exclusion of common sense. If a boat or sailboard that should give way to you fails to do so, shout! If it still refuses to respond, you will have to steer clear yourself.

Never play chicken with another boat or board. Sailboards are so manoeuvrable that there is no need to stick rigidly to the starboard tack just so that you can retain right of way.

If you do have right of way, however, you are obliged to keep a steady course and speed, so as not to confuse the other sailor. You should neither luff up nor bear away.

All changes of course should be made decisively, clearly and in good time.

Stay well away from boards that are

racing, so that you don't find yourself in a complicated right-of-way dilemma.

The fact is that boardsailing is a comparatively safe sport. But nevertheless there are more needless accidents than there should be, caused by high spirits, inexperience, overconfidence or faulty equipment. Anyone who has once seen the shore disappearing into the distance will be rather more careful next time. There is no substitute for experience. But to prevent you getting into difficulties in the first place, and so that you know what to do when faced with an emergency, you should study the following few rules so closely that they become second nature to you on the water.

An incident (not necessarily a collision) on a reservoir or gravel pit can be quickly resolved. On a larger lake or estuary, however, the situation can become critical very quickly; and on the coast it can herald disaster. Stick to the boardsailor's golden rule:

Treat the water with respect

As there is no place for a light on the mast of a sailboard — either a fixed one on the mast or a portable lamp in your hand — and as a compass is usually impractical, there is another rule that must be adhered to:

Never sail at night or in poor visibility

Make it a rule every time you go sailing to tell a friend of your plans. Give your destination and the time you expect to be back. If you alter your plans on the way, or if you fail to meet your timetable, try to let your friend know. Always take some money with you, so that you can telephone from a coinbox. This will prevent a false alarm and ensure that when you do need help you will get it.

Safety equipment

Ensure that all your equipment is in good shape and suitable for the kind of boardsailing you intend to do. It is no good taking a displacement or all round board into the Pacific rollers, but you can sail an all round funboard anywhere.

Mast leash

This is essential, even on a gravel pit in a Force 1. Every time you fall board and rig can go their separate ways; without a mast leash you may quickly find yourself in trouble.

A good mast leash should be strong enough to take a pull of 100 kilos from either board or rig, so a thin piece of shock cord with plastic hooks on the end is not good enough. Ideally you should make one for yourself out of 6mm line, made fast to the towing eye in the bow. The connection to the mast foot should be strong enough to take the required strain, but should also be easy to release, so that you can use the line as a tow rope if necessary.

Storm sail

Don't overrate your ability. From the shore the wind may often seem much weaker than it is in reality. If you are not absolutely certain that your normal sail will be OK, rig a smaller sail such as a storm sail. If, on the water, you decide that it is too small, you can always return to shore and change it. It is better to have to make a single sail change than to find yourself in trouble and helpless on the water.

Clothing

The look of your wet suit, its colour and its fashionable striping, are less important than its practicality. That is to say, in the first instance, it must keep you warm. If you are cold, you waste energy trying to warm yourself up, and may have insufficient reserves of energy to get you back to the shore.

The treacherous thing about exposure is that it begins slowly and almost imperceptibly. The first symptoms are a feeling of lethargy, muscle tremors, faster pulse and faster respiration. If the muscle tremors ease and your legs and arms begin slowly to stiffen up as you make your way to the shore, you are in real trouble. Signal for help immediately.

If help is unlikely to be immediately forthcoming, you must conserve your remaining store of energy. Don't, under any circumstances, carry on sailing; instead, sit on the board, arms and legs tucked into the body. Keep your clothing on.

When you are ashore and recovering, don't drink any alcohol.

Choose clothing with bright, even garish colours. If you have a white board and sail, and a black wet suit, it will be very difficult for a rescue team to find you. You should at least have a brightly-coloured, preferably red or orange, stripe on your sail or suit.

The mast leash may save your life. In strong winds a board freed from its rig will drift away faster than you can swim after it.

Emergency equipment

Special equipment

Unlike the dinghy sailor, the board-sailor cannot carry with him a set of spares, extra clothing or food. Learn trapeze sailing as soon as possible, as not only is this a less strenuous form of sailing that will enable you to reach the shore when the strength has left your muscles, but you will also have a little rucksack in which you can keep a whole range of bits and bobs that will come in useful if you get into difficulties.

The following is a recommended list of the basic minimum of equipment, which costs little, takes up very little space and which you should always carry with you:

● A trapeze harness should have a self-draining back pocket big enough for all your equipment, with some sort of rust-proof closure (nylon zip, or velcro fastening).

● Emergency line, at least two metres long and 6mm in diameter. It would be sensible to carry two other lines, each as long as the trapeze line.

● The best trapeze harness is useless if the hook breaks, so always take a spare hook.

● You will find that a roll of water-proof self-adhesive tape will be invaluable for all sorts of circumstances. You can always find a use for it.

● Some loose change for the tele-phone, glucose tablets and maybe some paper money kept in sealed poly-thene bag.

Essential for coastal sailboarding: an emergency equipment kit in your trapeze backpack.

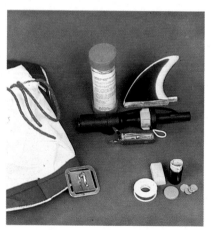

If you are going on a longer trip, perhaps out to sea, you should take with you a special equipment kit that will take up very little space and weigh less. In an emergency you may well need:

● Spare mast foot, in case yours breaks

● Pocket knife, with a small screwdriver

● Mini flares

● Spare fin

If you lose or break a fin it will be almost impossible to continue sailing. If your board has no centreboard and only one fin, you must carry a spare in your back pack.

If you check your kit every time you go sailing, your hobby will be safer and you can reduce the risks of the sport to a minimum. Boardsailing, in compari-son with some other sports, is a safe sport, if only you apply some common sense.

Self-help and International Distress Signals

Despite taking all possible precautions you may still find that you are within reach of the shore but unable to get there. You have no more strenght left, a sail that is too big, the wrong clothing — not warm enough —, a broken mast, a rising offshore wind and current; all could lead to an emergency. What do you do now?

Whatever happens next, remember and apply the following rules.

Keep calm, and don't leave your board

Even if you think you can make the bank by swimming, don't try. If you can't paddle there on your board, you won't reach it alone. So sit on your board, and think through your situation calmly and without panic. Can I help myself? How? Or will I need outside help?

If you can help yourself

If you have been driven offshore, it is usually due to wind, occasionally helped by the current. First of all determine the direction of drift. Find a point on the shore and watch it to see what direction you are heading in. It is almost impossible to estimate how far you being driven from the shore, so be sceptical about your observations. Then:

Choose not necessarily the shortest, but the most certain way of reaching the shore.

This means the way that requires least effort from you. Heading into wind or against the current is dangerous, as it will simply use up your remaining reserves of strength. Don't worry that it will mean a longer walk back to where you left your things; you will at least have terra firma under your feet.

If you should happen to lose your board — the worst of all emergencies — there will be nothing but to swim for it. But you should still avoid panicking.

No hectic crawl; just a gentle breast-stroke making use of the thrust of the waves. But once again, remember that the shortest way to shore is not necessarily the surest.

When you can no longer help yourself

Don't try to salve your pride when it comes to saving your life. Eschewing help because you are afraid of what your friends might say puts your own life at risk. Don't worry, either, about the cost of a call-out, because all the rescue organisations give their services free, though in some circum-

stances a rescuer might claim salvage rights over your board. But at least you will be safe.

You can call for help using what are known as the International Distress Signals: raise your arms above your head, lower them slowly to your side, and raise them again. Never use this signal to attract the attention of a friend; it may be misconstrued and you might find an unnecessary rescue mission launched on your behalf.

If you give a signal that has been acknowledged, but then find you can reach the shore on your own, you must make it clear that you no longer need help so that someone in greater need than you doesn't wallow helplessly while the rescuers make their way out to your side.

Towing: We have covered unrigging the board when out on the water. Lay the rolled-up rig on the board, and either hold on to the centreboard strap of the board which is towing you, or let it tow you by tying a line to the towing eye at the bow. The tow line is made fast with a bow-line to the mast of the board that is towing you.

If you are being towed by a fast boat, take the centreboard out, or the board will start shearing off first to one side, then to the other, and might even capsize and throw you into the water.

Helping others

It is not only important to know how to help yourself when you are in trouble. You should also know what to do if someone else needs your help.

Keep calm, once again. Don't leap straight into the water, but think through what you are going to do to rescue the other person. That way you won't unnecessarily put yourself at risk and make two casualties where previously there was only one.

First of all make sure that you are in a position to be able to help the other person — that it won't be too much for you. Beware of trying when the wind is too strong for you to rescue someone else. Also if the casualty is being pulled out to sea by a strong current and a relatively light wind you will be powerless to help unless you are a very competent sailor and know the local conditions.

Towing. You can only tow a board and sailor in winds of up to about Force 4 and in fairly calm water. Secure the tow line to the mast, to the centreboard strap or to the footstraps of your board. If you are starting off from the land, change the sail for a small one before you set off, as the water resistance of the two boards will be significantly higher and will therefore increase the pressure on the sail.

Bringing help. In an emergency you must act quickly and sensibly with due consideration of all the facts. It is best if you know the local conditions. It may profit to take with you when you go sailing the name, address and telephone number of someone who can help in an emergency — the local RNLI, the Coastguard, harbourmaster, police and so forth. But above all, it is vital that you describe the position accurately. This means covering the following points:

- Your own position.
- The time you saw the casualty.
- The bearing and distance of the casualty from the shore; be as accurate as possible.
- Nature of the emergency, so far as you can ascertain it.
- Description of the clothing of the person in trouble, his board and his sail.
- Your own name and where you can be contacted.

If after your emergency call you realise that the casualty is going to make it ashore on his own or with the help of someone else, be sure to cancel the alarm.

Four don'ts for boardsailors
- Don't go closer than 200 yards from a harbour entrance, moorings etc.
- Don't sail in a ship channel.
- Swimmers and bathers require special consideration. Boardsailors are subject to the same rules as other traffic on the water: they should not endanger, impede or inconvenience bathers.
- Don't go sailing at night or in reduced visibility.

PART II: BOARDSAILING FOR ADVANCED SAILORS

The fascination of boardsailing in strong winds

Boardsailing stands right at the top of the scale of fascinating modern sports. Most beginners dream of the day when they too will streak over the water like the experts, the sail raked to windward like a wing, hanging relaxed beneath it, apparently effortlessly, just above the waves. The board tears along like a water ski, the bow thumping quietly but aggressively on the rough water. At the stern there is a hissing noise, and the spray flies past as if you were being sprayed by a fire hose. You are planing.

Your enjoyment comes from a mixture of heady speed and an appreciation of things natural; sun, sparkling water, waves and wind.

Probably the most spectacular form of this young sport of boardsailing is sailing in strong winds, that is in winds of Force 4 and upwards. At Force 4 the wind blows at 11-16 knots, and that is just sufficient to get a sailboard to the point of planing, when it changes from sailing *in* the water, to sailing *over* the water.

For the beginner, who has just had a couple of hours teaching and now believes he can sail in any wind strength, Force 4 is a very difficult hurdle to conquer. In Force 3 winds, for example, the force of the wind on a normal 6m² sail amounts to about 17kg, a pressure which can be supported with muscle power. But wind pressure increases with the square of wind speed, — and even in a Force 4 wind, only one force higher, pressure on the sail is more than doubled to about 34kg. That is more than enough to pull a fully grown man off his feet, unless he counteracts it by using the weight of his body.

And that is the secret of strong wind sailing: to learn that you can lean back, right out over the water, without falling in; that the wish-bone boom, which transmits the driving force of the sail, also acts as a grab rail on which you can hang; that one has to establish equilibrium between wind force and the weight of one's body.

It normally takes 6-8 weekends training to overcome the strong wind hurdle. For sure, this will be accompanied by any number of unintentional swims: passing your swimming tests, the experts call it jokingly but with understanding because they too had to work their way through this stage themselves: climb on the board, fall in, and fall again — and again.

People watching and walking along the shore always find it amusing, just as they are fascinated when a skilled boardsailor whizzes past. It is probably due to this mixture of amusement and admiration that boardsailing has such a sympathetic image.

There are, of course, plenty of tips for those groping their way towards strong wind sailing: easiest and most energy-saving is certainly to sign on for a strong wind course in a boardsailing school. It is best to go for a course in an area where strong winds prevail so as to ensure that you have sufficient practical instruction. People who decide to teach themselves should preferably find a really small area of water, where waves will not grow too high in strong winds, because the higher the waves the more will the board be tossed about, and the more difficult will it be to handle the sail correctly. Having the right equipment also helps to make initial attempts easier.

Study the fascinating photos and see how easily the experts master the strong wind. How do they do it? They must be acrobats! — and fantastically strong. Of course, as in any sport, strength does come into it, but correct technique is far more important than muscles. And that I will deal with later in this book.

Particularly exciting is to surf using the ▶ *strength of the wind and the thrust of the waves.*

◀ *The secret of sailing in strong winds: lean right back over the water without falling in.*

Funboards — the boards for strong wind sailing

What is the attraction of strong wind sailing then? The answer is planing. You may have already heard it said that a lightweight vessel will either move in the displacement mode, or it will plane. A displacement boat is one which displaces a certain amount of water; she always sails *through* the water. On the other hand a planing boat, moving at higher speeds, lifts out of the water to travel *over* the surface.

When a displacement vessel moves through water, she meets two main types of resistance; there is form drag, caused by the nose pushing the water apart to make room for the underwater body, and frictional resistance which arises when water molecules slide past the whole of the wetted area. Frictional resistance is almost eliminated

A round displacement-type board points well and sails fast.

Flat planing boards are easy to sail and very fast in strong winds.

when a vessel planes, because when the boat or board lifts onto the surface to skim over the water, the wetted area is decreased, and friction is reduced proportionally. Out on the water the effect is immediately noticeable because the braking effect of the water decreases as the board lifts from displacement sailing to planing, and the board accelerates suddenly although pressure on the sail remains unchanged.

Since planing is what delights people about strong wind sailing, boardsailors and designers have developed a board which lifts more easily out of the water, thus enormously increasing the speed attainable. This is the **Funboard**, which has a flat planing bottom, but only really gets going in Force 4 and above, when the wind blows hard enough to make it plane.

Calling this board a Funboard does not mean that you would have no fun with a normal Allround board, but rather that you could sail much faster in a strong wind, without great exertion, than when sailing on a larger displacement board. With the higher speed come new and exciting possibilities; the board can be swung back and forth, even in short waves, using a motion similar to wedeling on skis.

Recently board design has advanced rapidly from the days when boardsailing fanatics had to make do with allround boards, whether they were sailing inland or in surf; today, however, there is a special board for every purpose: racing boards for open classes, racing boards for funboard racing, short manoeuvrable boards for surf, narrow boards for high speed sailing, and many more.

Side by side with specialised boards, there has been the gradual development of a type of board that covers 80 per cent of the spectrum of board-sailors' needs. This new generation of boards is the answer for all those who do not want a different board for every different type of water, but one board which will be treat to sail in as many different areas and in as varied conditions as possible. Generally only one extra is needed, over and above the basic equipment supplied with the board, and that is a small sail for use in strong winds.

It has taken designers a considerable time to meet the requirements of these boardsailors, but today it is boards of this type, the Allround-Funboards and Funboards, that dominate the scene. If you intend to sail in strong winds, I would advise you, every time, to buy such a board.

Above Force 4, conditions vary of course, and Funboards can therefore be divided into three main groups:

1. Allround Funboards
2. Short Funboards
3. Race Funboards

Theoretically boards designed for maximum speed could be classed as short Funboards; they are mostly Sinkers.

Allround Funboards are a good compromise board for beginners and sailing inland. Novices can learn on them, but they perform well in strong winds too.

Allround-Funboards

Allround-Funboards are the most versatile, because they can be sailed in winds from Force 0-6. Their length of 3.50-3.70m makes them directionally stable, while their beam of 650-700mm gives them lateral stability. Thus they can be used by beginners, too, when the wind is light.

If your intention is to learn the technique of sailing Funboards, this board is the right answer, but it should have removable foot straps, a fully retractable centreboard and the possibility of fitting a variety of fins.

Due to their shape, Allround Funboards
are very quick to start planing.

Short Funboards

Short funboards are suitable only for experts because they are very wobbly, due to the short length of 2.00-3.40m and 500-650mm beam. Nor do they always have sufficient buoyant volume to keep the boardsailor plus his clothing and the rig afloat on the surface. There are three sizes: Floaters, Semi-sinkers and Sinkers.

Floaters. With a buoyant volume of about 140-200 litres, a board will support a boardsailor and his equipment without sinking. Sinkers are classed among larger boards on account of their 3.00-3.40m length.

Semi-sinkers. With 90-130 litres buoyant volume, you can stand on the board to raise the sail out of the water, but the board will readily dip beneath the surface. If you fail to stand bang in the centre and keep the board balanced, the nose or the tail will sink below water. Given its length of 2.60-3.00m, the semi-sinker is considerably more difficult to handle.

Sinker. The shortest and smallest boards, with a length of about 2.00-2.60m and a buoyant volume of under 90 litres, are the Sinkers. When boardsailors stand on them to raise the sail from the water, they sink beneath the surface; the only method of getting under way is therefore the Waterstart, which is described on p.112 — Advanced Boardsailing; these boards are only suitable for the relatively few who are expert. Naturally the weight of the boardsailor plays a part; a board which a 65kg boardsailor would call a semi-sinker would be a sinker to an 80kg man.

Three types of short Funboard: left, a Floater which has sufficient buoyancy for the sail to be raised; centre, a Semi-sinker, only occasionally can the sail be raised; right, a Sinker — you have to make a waterstart to get under way.

Although Sinkers and Semi-sinkers are difficult to sail, they shift at an intoxicating speed in strong winds, and are fantastically manoeuvrable.

Regatta Funboards

The third type of high-wind board, the regatta funboard, is sometimes called a 'Gun'. It was developed specifically for funboard regattas. Because of the different disciplines and varying wind strengths in these regattas, these are relatively long boards (3.70-3.90m) but in spite of this they are not particularly stable as they are rarely more than 0.6m wide. This narrowness above all increases speed on offwind legs of the course. The volume of the board is only 200-230 litres to save weight. All these speed boards are fitted with centreboards about 0.6-0.7m long for good upwind sailing performance. The centreboard can be raised for reaching and running legs. They are not suitable for beginners, understandably, being a specialised hybrid for particular conditions and racing — but very exciting!

Racing Funboards are always a compromise; allround performance is good, and strong wind qualities are first class. They point well, and sail with little fuss, but rapid tacking and gybing is more difficult than with shorter boards.

Which board to choose

The comfort rig for strong winds

There are no hard and fast rules as to which type of board is fastest. Each is designed for specific wind and wave conditions, based on the scientific analysis of practical experience.

Experts who are hot on physics as well as boardsailing generally decide themselves on the shape of their boards. They either make these Custom boards themselves or employ a specialist who shapes them as required.

Before buying a board, first ask yourself how committed to the sport are you going to be. If you expect to be a casual boardsailor who goes out for a spin now and then at weekends, I would recommend an Allround board which performs best in light to moderate winds.

On the other hand if you intend to get stuck into strong wind sailing immediately you have passed the beginner's stage, there is no doubt that what you need is an Allround-Funboard or a Funboard with which you will have no problems when you enjoy the excitement of sailing at high speed in strong winds.

The Sail

It may be that you are lucky enough to own an Allround-Funboard or a Funboard already, or perhaps have the opportunity to borrow one.

But there is more to it than just a light board with a bottom shaped for planing and a sharp trailing edge, because you also need a suitable rig, good fins, and a slight change in your sailing technique.

You can use your normal rig initially, but after a few attempts you will find that you have a problem. The board's Centre of Lateral Resistance shifts considerably further aft when you plane, and you therefore have to shift your rig further aft too to maintain equilibrium. When you are moving really fast, your rig will be raked so far aft that the end of the boom will suddenly dip into the water and you, sailing at full speed, will be thrown off.

The answer is the High-Clew sail which, in particular, is cut with a clew that is higher than usual; this makes sail handling rather easier. Less effort

is required to raise this rig when starting because the water runs off so quickly, and even when the mast is raked sharply aft, the boom end does not dip beneath the surface. Nor will it catch on the face of a wave when you are sailing in strong winds and steep seas.

The Maui sail, named after the Hawaiian island of Maui, is typical of this cut. The mast and boom are short, but the sail is broad near the head and extended by battens. Nowadays the fully-battened sail is becoming ever

more popular. With its snug fitting mast sleeve, the battens press so firmly against the mast that the sail takes up an aerofoil shape even when there is no wind. It curves smoothly to leeward, with no belly just aft of the mast, and airflow adhesion is optimum. The aerofoil shape extends right to the foot, which also has a definite curve. The result is a sail shaped like a wing and, despite the shorter boom, greater drive.

There are four different sizes of sail at present. The wind strength at which

Fast planing over smooth water is the ultimate fascination for the boardsailor. Given the right conditions and commitment you can learn in half a season.

they will be used depends upon the ability of the individual boardsailor. The large sail is 5.60-6.00m² in area; the medium sail about 5.00m²; the All round sail is 4.60m²; the storm sail is 4.00m².

The mast

The Boom

It is no good spending money on an expensive sail of the highest quality if it doesn't match your mast and boom. You should ideally therefore take your mast with you when you buy a sail so that you can see whether the curvature of the mast matches the curve cut of the sail. If you have a hard rig, your sail will keep its shape, in strong winds in particular.

Hard aluminium masts are certainly not the answer for jumping in waves and surf because of the considerable force with which the board lands, and a hard mast will break sooner due to the great stresses which arise in surf. It is essential to reinforce the mast at the foot and where the boom is attached.

There is no point in having a foot extension or an adjustable mast foot that can be raised unless you have several sails to set on the same mast. If the height from the tack to the deck is right, 300-500mm, there is usually no need for further adjustment.

A small cleat should always be fitted to the mast foot so that the downhaul can be made fast and released quickly.

The distance between the wishbones should not be too great because otherwise your back will brush the water when you pull the rig right back to windward. However there is no point in having a narrow boom if the wishbones are so soft and they bend outwards when under load. It is therefore preferable to have a rather heavier but stiffer boom.

The sheathing should not be too rough, and it must be glued firmly to the wishbones.

A short boom, 2.00-2.20m long is essential for a comfort rig. Longer wishbone booms are required for a larger racing funsail about 7.00m^2 in area and for Allround-Funboards in light winds.

The tack should be about 300mm above the deck; it is easier to make the downhaul fast in a cleat.

Design details of strong wind boards

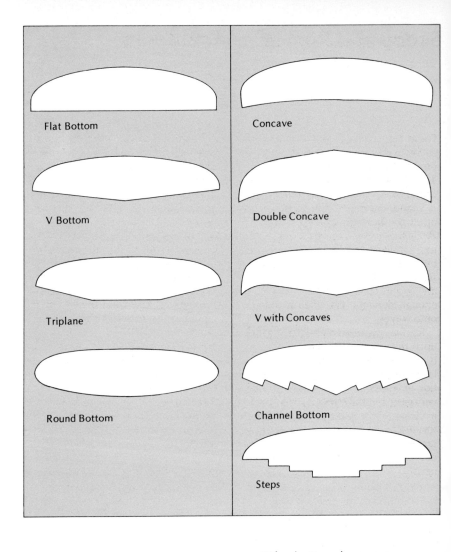

Flat Bottom

V Bottom

Triplane

Round Bottom

Concave

Double Concave

V with Concaves

Channel Bottom

Steps

The Bottom

The decisive factor which governs the sailing characteristics of the board is the bottom on which the board slides over the water.

The four main shapes are:

Flat bottom: planes quickly, the basic shape.

V-bottom: good near the tail for foot steering and to avoid Spin Out.

Triplane: similar to the V-bottom, but planes sooner owing to the flat central part.

Round bottom: the rails are no more than 300mm above the deepest point, so the curve is very small, gentle entry of the rails into the water.

Nobody has yet found the optimum shape. The aim is always to find the most satisfactory combination of planing ability, directional stability and manoeuvrability by using a combination of these shapes.

Other bottom shapes are:

Concave: gives great lift and, up to a point, good direction.

Double Concave: similar to Concave, but possibly even more effective.

V with Concave: better grip at the rail, but good lift too.

Channel bottom: provides better lateral grip.

Steps: reduces the wetted area when speed increases.

Scoop and Rocker   Rails

These terms relate to the degree of curve in the planing surfaces of the board at bow and stem, fore and aft. They have a very considerable effect on the board's sailing characteristics.

Scoop, the degree the board bends up at the bow, generally amounts to 200-300mm; the curve upwards starts just forward of the mast foot and becomes progressively greater. It is steepest at the bow to discourage nose diving and to provide the board with enough dynamic lift when it thumps onto waves.

Rocker, the degree the board bends up at the stern, either starts well aft or is spread over the whole board. The latter provides a better planing position in waves, and also makes turning very easy, but the effect is unfortunate in strong winds and calm water when the braking effect of the form resistance resulting from the curvature causes the board to see-saw continuously.

A board which has sharp rails at the bow will cut through the water and be difficult to control. All that part of the board that is forward of the position of the Centre of Lateral Resistance at higher speed should have rounded rails.

It is the shape of the rails that largely controls a board's sailing characteristics. A number of alternative shapes are used:

Soft Rail: the radius is the same throughout; runs from the bow to the centre of the board for easy manoeuvrability.

Tucked Under Edge: the radius is like Soft Rail, but there is a kink in the lower part which assists the water to break away cleanly.

Box: no good for the rails because manoeuvrability is impaired. Can however be used at the stern to improve pointing.

Down Soft Rail: the radius of the upper

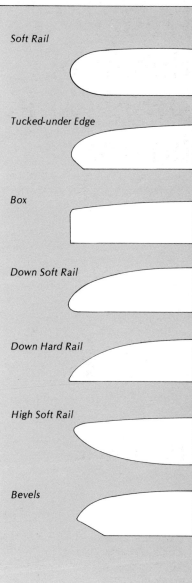

Soft Rail

Tucked-under Edge

Box

Down Soft Rail

Down Hard Rail

High Soft Rail

Bevels

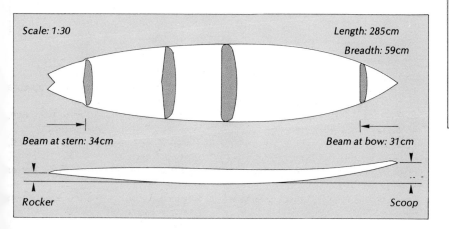

Scale: 1:30

Length: 285cm

Breadth: 59cm

Beam at stern: 34cm

Beam at bow: 31cm

Rocker

Scoop

99

curve is greater than that of the lower; when used near the stern, improves directional stability.

Down Hard Rail: provides still better lateral control. With the sharp rail, water breaks away cleanly at the stern.

High Soft Rail: Turning qualities are improved at the expense of directional ' stability; broader deck, Used only between the bow and the mast foot.

Bevels: become gradually narrower, and end where the planing surface starts. The board turns more easily and the wetted area is reduced when planing.

Various shapes can be combined. When a single shape is used throughout, there are usually disadvantages whereas, for example, the combination of Down Soft Rails forward with Down Hard Rails aft provides a balanced mixture of manoeuvrability and directional stability.

Sterns

The bottom and the rails are not the only factors to affect a board's sailing characteristics; the type of stern plays a big part too because it alters the length of the surface on which the board planes, and consequently its speed. In particular the type of stern affects a board's manoeuvrability.

For a start, there are broad sterns and narrow sterns. With a broad stern a board will start to plane earlier, but you lose out on manoeuvrability, and there is a tendency to spin out at high speeds. A board with a narrow stern, on the other hand, is slower to plane but can be controlled well, even at high speeds.

Which type of shape to choose

The various stern shapes result in different sailing characteristics. Generally, broader sterns plane more readily, and narrower sterns slip through the water more quietly. A board turns easier if the stern curves slightly upwards (rocker).

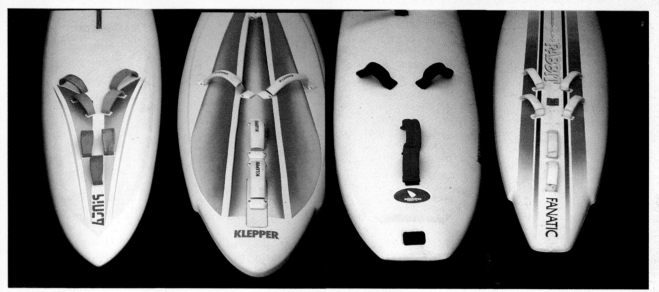

| Pintail | Pintail Winger | Squashtail | Squashtail Winger |

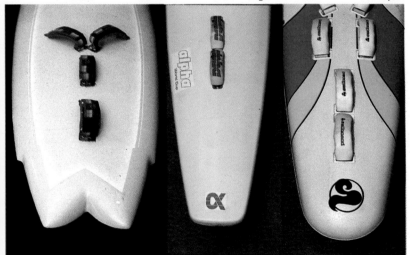

| Swallowtail Winger | Square tail | Round tail |

Although they break the smoothness of the curve, the board is slightly widened which enables it to plane earlier. The rail also has a better grip when tacking and gybing quickly, because they act like little fins when forced down into the water.

The Squashtail has a rather broader stern which guarantees excellent jumping qualities because you can push off even from smaller waves. The drawback is that it is rather restless when gybing quickly.

The *Squashtail Winger* is equally suitable for jumping, and relatively good turning characteristics result from the rather narrower stern.

The *Swallowtail* is a combination of a Squashtail and two small Pintails. Good planing characteristics and good push off when jumping are assured by the relatively beamy stern, while the small pintails either side provide better grip when turning.

The *Squaretail*, with its large wetted area, planes well and its broad tail provides a good surface for jumping. The

depends on the sailor's individual style and on the area where he will sail. The following are some of the shapes available.

Pintail: Curves smoothly right to the tail. Waterflow is attached and there is no disturbance before it breaks away; this makes the shape particularly suitable for higher waves. Given narrow rails, especially near the stern, the board is very manoeuvrable, and will grip the face of a wave well.

The *Pintail Winger* has small fin-like corners either side, close to the stern.

disadvantages are that the board does not turn so readily and that it is more likely to spin out.

If the board is to be used mainly in winds of Force 4 to 5, the *Roundtail* is a good compromise in that it turns better, but in stronger winds a Roundtail does not sail quietly, and tends to spin out.

Another trend in boards came from Hawaii; these are what are called asymmetric boards. They were developed in answer to a problem which is ever-present when waves are large; on the one hand enough buoyancy is required to work out through the surf, while on the other hand the board has to be completely under control so as to be fully manoeuvrable while wave-riding. Thus a rather broader stern, such as a Squashtail, is the answer when sailing out, whereas the Pintail is better for wave-riding because the board must

always be under control and react instantly to foot steering on account of the great speeds achieved. The solution, then, is to combine both shapes in one board.

A board of this type is naturally suited only to very specific waters. If the wind is blowing from your right when you look seaward from the shore, you will sail out on starboard tack, and the left hand side of the board must be wider. This is also helpful if you have to sail slightly closer to the wind when sailing out because, even at slower speeds, the broader stern helps the board to plane earlier. When you are far enough offshore, you gybe and sail back in, riding the waves on port tack. Now you need to be able to bear away in a flash to accelerate or to meet a wave, and if the right side of the board is narrower, you can turn the board in a tighter arc.

Asymmetric boards are suitable only in waters where the wind always blows from the same direction.

This board combines the Pintail with the Squashtail. The broader half helps the board to plane earlier when sailing out against the waves; the narrower half increases its manoeuvrability when riding the waves back to the shore.

The centreboard

The centreboard is not always one of the essential components of a strong wind board, because the fins of Funboards often take over its function.

We know already that a centreboard is not required on a beam reach, so the only sensible type is a vario centreboard which is fully retractable, but which can be lowered for beating. Flexible watertight seals reduce the resistance caused by the long centreboard case. The centreboard must lock into place effectively so that it does not drop every time the board thumps down on a wave, and it should be easy to manipulate with your feet.

In strong winds its weight is less important than its strength, and wooden centreboards have proved efficient, as have polypropylene centreboards.

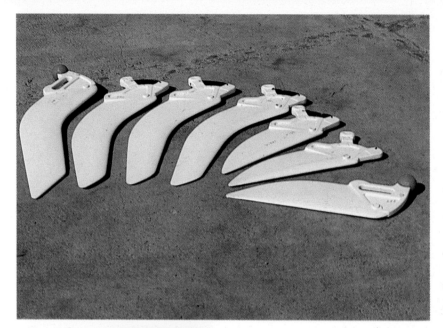

Different centreboard shapes for use in varying wind strengths. Left, larger centreboards for light winds and pointing close to the wind; right, storm centreboards.

Centreboard seals prevent water from squirting up into the centreboard case.

If the centreboard stands proud of the deck, cushioning prevents the sharp trailing edge from injuring your feet.

Fins and fin cases

The role of the fin has become more and more important as boards become smaller and consequently faster. Its shape, profile and position all affect the board's behaviour.

The American 8mm wide fin case, developed from surfboards, is the most widely used, but because a sailboard fin is subject to greater loads, a deeper case is needed to take the greater lateral force.

There is relatively little pressure on an Allround board's fin, because its purpose is merely to provide directional stability, but it is a very different matter with Funboards where the fin often takes over the function of the centreboard; not only must its lateral area be sufficient to prevent the board from luffing up, but it must also discourage 'spin out'.

Yes, spin out; you may well already have experienced this at some time. It happens when you are, sailing

There are almost as many different fin shapes as there are board shapes. Fin and board must match each other well.

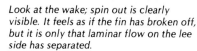

Look at the wake; spin out is clearly visible. It feels as if the fin has broken off, but it is only that laminar flow on the lee side has separated.

extremely fast; the stern suddenly lurches off to leeward, the board slows dramatically and swings round at right angles and you describe a graceful arc through the air as you are flung into the water.

There are two theories as to what causes spin out; the first is ventilation, which occurs when air is drawn beneath the moving board as it churns up the water. Low pressure at the fin sucks the air downwards until it reaches the tip; the fin is then surrounded by air, not water.

Cavitation, the second theory, is also associated with low pressure caused by the streamlining of the fin. On occasion this effect can be so great that the water beside the fin starts to boil (it is a well-known fact that when pressure is very low water boils at a temperature of well under 100°.) Steam forms and is as unsatisfactory a medium for the fin to work in as air. Both effects probably contribute to spin out.

Efforts to reduce this problem affect other handling characteristics; the larger the fin, both in area and in depth, the faster can the board sail before spin off occurs, but the less manoeuvrable will the board be.

Fins underwater. A trapezoidal fin helps the board to point high, whereas with a sabre-shaped fin it will turn more readily.

Another way to avoid spin out is to fit fences; these horizontal ledges round the fin are fitted to prevent the air from being sucked down. There is no conclusive proof that these fiddly additions are a real cure.

The same can be said of Tracker fins which are asymmetric, being straight on one side and curved on the other. They are fitted in pairs and when water

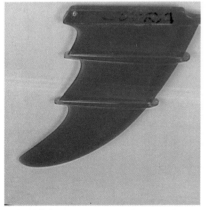

Fin with fences prevents spin out.

flows past pressure is high on the flat inner side and low on the curved outer side. When the board is lying flat on the water, the forces on the two fins cancel each other out.

The correct compromise is what is required for every type of board. One with a broad stern, for example, needs greater fin area, but a fin over 250mm long develops so much lift at the stern that the board would tend to capsize, and the lateral area required is therefore better distributed between two or three smaller fins. This can be done in three ways.

● The single fin, which is used mostly on modern Pintails and Racing Boards.

● The twin fin layout, which is best for Roundtails, Squashtails and similar shapes.

● The Thruster combination of two side fins which are generally smaller than the central guiding fin fitted further aft. The great advantage of this layout is that the fin on the inside of the curve never leaves the water, even in the tightest of turns.

As to the question of material, most American fins are laminates made of several layers of woven glass. They are extraordinarily hard and durable but are rarely fully streamlined because the leading and trailing edges are not properly rounded.

European fins are mostly made of spray moulded Lexan. They are perfectly streamlined and relatively cheap, but break more easily. However it is often better to buy a new fin than to have to repair a fin case that has been wrenched out.

The cheapest fins are made of a thermoplastic material such as polyethylene or polypropylene. Although most are well streamlined, they are relatively soft and dent easily, which affects water flow adversely.

Footstraps

(left) Single fin (centre) Twin fins (bottom) Thruster layout

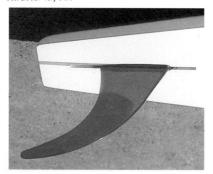

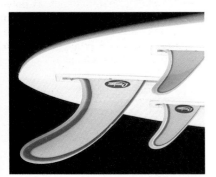

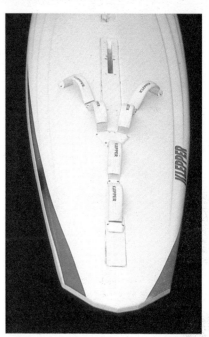

Allround-Funboard, six straps.

Whereas it used to be only a few of the most expert boardsailors who fitted footstraps, nowadays even beginners start to use them as soon as they have learnt basic techniques.

They have several uses. First they improve your control of the board because your footing is more sure. Then they prevent your parting company with the board when you are jumping. Most important of all, though, is that they make it possible to use a completely different technique from what you learnt initially, because when you sail a Funboard in a strong wind, you do not steer by raking the rig, but by shifting your weight and tilting the board sideways with your feet in the footstraps.

The position of the footstraps depends on the type of board, and the ability and style of the boardsailor. Initially you should fit the forward straps at an angle of about 45° to the centreline, 400-500mm aft of the mast foot. You can either fit the aft straps on the centreline, so that you can use them on both tacks, or parallel to each other.

Usually two pairs of straps are fitted forward to Allround-Funboards, and two or three straps aft. The forward pair are for light winds and close or beam reaching, and the after pair are used when sailing fast on a broad reach. The number and position depends on the size of the board. For a Floater over 3m in length, the recommended strap layout is the same as for

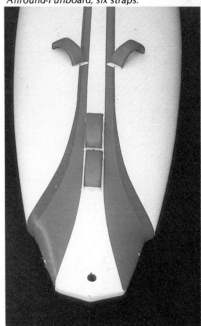

Funboard, four straps.

Many straps for tacking and gybing.

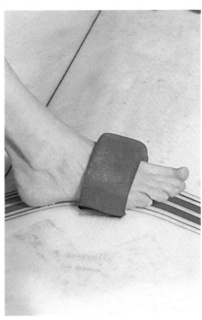

Dangerous — the strap is too long.

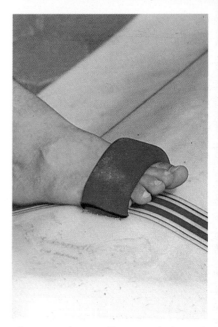

Correct — the strap fits across the base of the toes.

A row of footstraps on a narrow board.

Allround-Funboards.

One pair of straps forward and a single strap aft is the usual system for very short boards. An extra strap in the centre is useful for wave-riding to enable you to thrust with your knees, and also to gybe tightly.

Footstraps on very narrow boards are all fitted fore-and-aft on the centre-line.

A greater number of footstraps are required for long racing boards to enable you to stand in the best position on all points of sailing, whatever the wind strength.

It is particularly important that foot-straps should be the right size for you, and the rule to follow to avoid injury is this: when you push your foot into the strap, only your toes should be visible on the far side. If the straps are too long, your foot could slip through right up to the shin. When you fall it is very difficult to extricate your leg while lying on your back in the water, attached to the board — and that can be dangerous.

Footstraps are essential for controlled jumping.

Mast track

Originally mast tracks were fitted to enable racing boards to sail faster and point higher, but now tracks have even been fitted to semi-sinkers so that a board's directional stability and manoeuvrability can be altered in a second or two. This eliminates, to

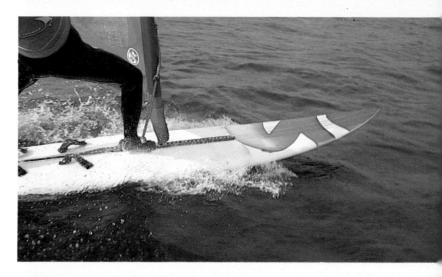

Mast traveller forward; the boom is thrust downwards.

Mast traveller aft; pull the mast aft with you mast hand.

Tracks vary enormously; the essential is that the traveller should slide easily.

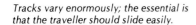

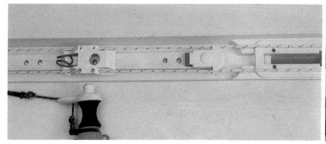

some extent at least, the nuisance of the mast foot being in the wrong position.

The rubber universal joint is mounted on a traveller, which slides on a track fitted along the centreline. The traveller can be locked at whatever notch in the track is required so as to trim the board correctly. Some tracks have holes into which the traveller clicks.

There is one difficulty, however. There is generally a rubber strap which pulls the traveller back when you release a catch. If you want to shift the rig further aft, you use your strength to pull the boom towards the stern. It should be possible to work the mechanism with your foot, but the track is usually gummed up with sand and salt and you almost always have to bend down and manually shift the traveller which carries the rig.

A board with a mast foot on a track will point higher when the mast is shifted further forward. The rig can then be carried more upright, and waterline length is increased because the bow is lower. On the reach, however, when wetted area should be as small as possible to reduce frictional resistance, and lateral area is no longer required to restrict leeway, taking the rig as far aft as possible lifts the bow above the water and cuts down the wetted surface area.

A track can be useful in semi-sinkers too. It is considerably easier to pull the rig out of the water when the traveller is pulled aft to the broadest part of the board. You then thrust the mast foot forward towards the bow to the best position for sailing at speed before getting under way. When the mast foot is forward the board will not turn so readily of course, so you have to pull it right aft if you want to do power gybes and tight turns.

Board trim

Anyone who has sailed an Allround board in winds of Force 4 or more will know all about it; when you harden in the sail, the nose of the board turns inexorably towards the wind, you are pushed sideways through the water for a while and then generally find yourself swimming. Designers have been making boards which are ever more suitable for strong winds so as to counter this unpleasant tendency.

What is it that happens when you sail at high speed in a strong wind? The board's bow lifts ever further out of the water, and this causes a reduction in the lateral area, particularly forward, while the centre of lateral resistance shifts further aft. The board-sailor has to rake his rig aft too, to keep the forces in equilibrium.

On the fastest points of sailing, that is beam reaching and broad reaching, the centreboard is no longer needed to prevent leeway, and it is therefore raised within the board. This also reduces the lateral area drastically in the centre of the board, the CLR wanders further aft, and you have to take another step aft, raking the sail aft at the same time.

The fact that the centreboard is withdrawn into the board reduces the wetted area and, with that, frictional resistance. The board therefore accelerates, the bow lifts higher out of the water, the CLR moves further aft, and you have to take another step back.

The aim is to establish optimum trim for every point of sailing at whatever speed you are moving. In order to balance the forces, you can shift the centreboard, fit a different shape of fin, and move the centre of the forces which act on the sail (the centre of effort) and the centre through which the braking forces act (the centre of lateral resistance) further forward or aft...

It is easier to trim the board perfectly if you have a mast track so that you can shift your rig towards the bow or stern.

Basically your board should be trimmed so that balance is neutral, and therefore has no tendency to luff up or bear away, because you do not wish to expend your energy on resisting a continual tendency to turn; this makes you very tense and would spoil the fun of sailing in strong winds.

Advanced Boardsailing

Sailing with a harness

When sailing on a lovely day with a Force 5 wind, it is a pity if you have to drop your rig in the water after ten minutes or so because of cramp in your forearms. You sit and massage your muscles, bemoan the fact that you are not fit enough, and envy the people you can see fizzing past effortlessly, hour after hour, hanging relaxed in a harness.

It is a fact that someone who has mastered the art of sailing with a harness does not only conserve his strength and keep going for longer; he also sails better because he can pay attention to board trim instead of concentrating on hanging on to the boom. Sailing becomes even more fun when you plane effortlessly over the water. Furthermore many people boardsailing at sea have only made it back to land because their reserves of strength lasted out thanks to wearing harnesses. harnesses.

I am starting this section on sailing technique for advanced boardsailors with the harness because I believe it makes sailing in strong winds so much more fun. Furthermore it eliminates the frustration of 'overstretched arms'.

But everyone new to sailing with

Sailing with a harness makes boardsailing considerably safer, as well as allowing you to enjoy yourself longer in strong winds.

You can steer the board just as precisely when wearing a harness.

harness will have doubts — in theory at least — about safety. What happens if I cannot unhook myself when I fall? or if I am under the sail and the harness is still hooked on? or if the lines get twisted when I am catapulted off?

These are justifiable doubts but, given correctly used gear, a little practice and some skill, such problems are solved because the harness line normally releases itself as you fall; if not, you can stroke it out of the hook with a single movement when lying in the water.

The vital point is this: never panic, stay calm.

If you decide to get a harness, check a few points before buying it:

● *Does it fit?* The back should not cut into or chafe your shoulders or arms. The straps must be long enough for the hook to lie roughly at the bottom of your breastbone, but should be adjust-

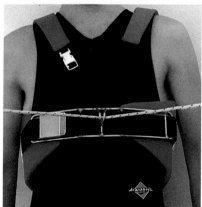

With a broad base plate for the hook the load is carried by your back without constricting your chest.

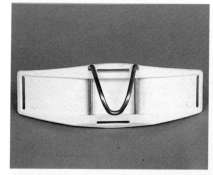

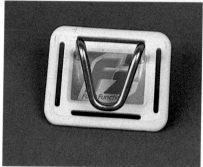

A rope that gets twisted round a conical hook will drop off automatically.

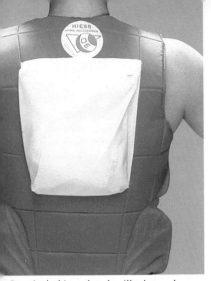

Practical: this rucksack will take car keys, money and a safety pack.

The harness lines are best attached to the booms about a shoulders' breadth apart.

Figure of eight knot; make the harness lines fast like this.

able so that it can be moved up and down when others use the harness.

● *Has the belt a quick release clasp?* This can be released if, for example, you have twisted round in a catapult fall and are lying under the sail. A quickly operated clasp is also preferable when putting on the harness.

● *Does the base plate of the hook extend right across your chest?* Only then can the load be transmitted to your back without constricting your chest.

● *Is the hook conical?* If so, a rope that has wrapped itself around it when you fall will drop off automatically.

● *Are there four slots in the baseplate to feed the straps through?* If not, you cannot shift the hook up and down.

● *Has it got a rucksack?* This is extraordinarily useful for carrying spare lines, wax, money, car keys — even a storm sail if the rucksack is large enough.

The straps should fit snugly, and should be made of a material that is not too soft, because they will hurt after a short while if they curl up under load. It is best to put the harness on in the shop and hang in it for several minutes somewhere so as to check all these points.

Before you set out on the water, avoid being disappointed initially by carefully adjusting the straps so that the wind force acts neutrally on your body. This means making the harness lines fast to the boom at the correct place so as to distribute the pull equally between your two hands.

The best method is to set up the rig on the beach, harden in the sail, and gradually move your hands towards each other. They meet at the centre point where the rig is balanced. This point is midway between the places where you make the ends of the harness lines fast. Use 6mm rope, about 1.20-1.50m long, and attach one line to each wishbone boom using a figure of eight knot through which you pass the other end of the line, upwards. This makes a loop which will pull really tight around the boom, but which you can release very easily when you wish.

When the wind increases you generally need to shift the harness lines away from the mast so as to move the centre of effort further aft, and if you make your lines fast with a knot which cannot be slacked off instantly, such as a rolling hitch, you will find it almost impossible to do this on the water.

It is entirely up to you as to whether you grip the boom out-side, on, or in-side the knots. Find out which suits you best, and adjust your lines accordingly.

The time still has not come to storm out on to the water; first practise hooking on and unhooking yourself again on land. Put on the harness, set the rig up in sand or on a pier, and harden in the sail. Hook yourself on by swinging the line down and up towards you with the boom. The essential point is to pull the boom towards you rather than leaning your body towards the boom.

As soon as the rope is in the hook, lean back until you feel pressure on the harness. Slowly and gradually transfer the pull from your hands to the harness and your back. Do not be afraid to lean right back — wind pressure will support you. Now try to keep the rig balanced for at least ten minutes, leaving your hands lying slack on the boom.

When wind pressure increases in a gust, lean further back and bend your knees slightly to lower your centre of gravity. When the gust eases, bend

This is how to find the right position for attaching the harness lines; gradually

move your hands along the boom towards each other to find the centre of effort. To

balance the rig, the centre of the harness line has to be opposite this point.

your trunk forward slightly and harden the sail for a moment to avoid falling backwards.

Now try unhooking yourself; just pull the boom towards you with a jerk, and the harness line will drop out of the hook as soon as it is slack. Practise hooking on and unhooking yourself a number of times until you are really confident.

At last the time has come to go out on the water, preferably on a warm sunny day with a Force 2 or 3 wind and smooth water so that you can control your board without any difficulty; you will then be free to concentrate on your harness. Go far enough offshore to avoid disturbing anyone, and hook on just as you have been practising on land. Gradually transfer the sail pressure from your arms to the harness, and try to lean back just far enough for the weight of your body to balance the wind force.

You can use your feet effectively to steer the board now; hardening the sail in briefly with your sail hand puts pressure on your forward foot, and the board will bear away. A quick thrust with your back foot and the board will luff up again. Raking the rig slightly forward or aft helps the board to alter course, and the hook will slide back and forth along the harness line as you do so.

Now try out the harness on all points of sailing; only the position of your feet changes as you do so. You will find for sure that you will fail to lean far enough back when a gust strikes, and will suddenly be jerked to leeward by the sail. In the normal way you would just drop the boom, but you cannot do this when you are hooked on and unable to free yourself quickly. This is a stupid fall, which looks rather comic because you plump helplessly into the sail. However there is no danger whatsoever; just keep hold of the boom to avoid hitting your chest or neck on it as you fall. The harness line will generally drop out of the hook of its own accord, so all you have to do is to push yourself up on the mast or the sail and clamber back on board.

The way to avoid falling like this? React quickly beforehand; at the right moment either lean back to windward or ease out the sail.

Once you have become accustomed to the harness in Force 2-3 winds, you can try it when it is blowing harder. Your strength will be no problem because the harness takes so much work from your arms, but you have to compensate by being that much more skilful. After starting on a beam reach, hook yourself on in the usual way and then find the most comfortable position — with your legs slightly bent and your hands, relaxed, lying on the boom ready to make such corrections as are needed for altering course. You deal with gusts exactly the same way as you would when not wearing a harness, by either leaning back to windward or easing out the sail.

Stay hooked on when you ease out the sail by pushing the boom away with your sail hand and pulling it towards you with your mast hand; the hook will slide forward along the line. You will feel rather insecure, and the best answer is to harden in again immediately so that you can, so to speak, support yourself with the pressure in the sail. When the wind eases suddenly, counter by hardening in the sail with a jerk and, if that is insufficient, by thrusting your knees forward.

As soon as the first stage is behind you, you will experience a completely new sensation. Instead of having to concentrate on holding on, and having to change course frequently to ease the load on your arms, you simply lean back as if you were in a rocking chair, and enjoy the real pleasure of board-sailing for the first time.

But what happens when you cannot counter the pressure and the strong wind simply tears you off the board, or when a gust ceases so abruptly that you fall beneath the sail still hooked on? Nothing much, actually; just let yourself fall and stay calm — do not panic. As soon as the pressure is out of the sail, stroke the line down out of the hook with one hand. That is all you need to do, and it only takes a fraction of a second.

It is not until you are whipped into a catapult when wearing a harness that you discover how great are the forces involved. You are catapulted forward with absolutely irresistable power and will generally land in the water between the mast and the board, although sometimes you fly into the sail. Again, stay calm, grab the hook, push the line down, and surface.

The only time it could be more difficult is when the wind turns you round your own harness line while catapulting you forward through the air, and you then land beneath the sail. Normally you can still unhook yourself with one hand, but if you find you cannot for some reason or other (I have never heard of this happening), open the quick release clasp and disconnect yourself entirely. There can be no difficulty if your hook is conical because when a hook is this shape a line under load will automatically be pulled off.

All in all, the harness is the most sensible extra for boardsailing because, by helping to conserve energy, it opens up the true delights of relaxed planing. You will not sail faster if you use a harness, but your pleasure will certainly increase.

Many inventors and gadget-makers have designed systems to make harnesses even more pleasant, and in particular, even safer than the Hawaii harness, as it is called, but so far none of these usually more complicated systems has really caught on. The success of the Hawaii harness is possibly due to its simplicity and to the fact that it is not dangerous. Up to now no boardsailing accident has been attributed to the use of harness; equally no one knows how many serious accidents could have been avoided if one had been used.

Starting in a strong wind

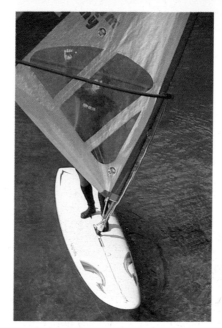

Even if you can keep your balance on the board relatively well, you will find that starting when the wind is blowing hard can produce plenty of problems if your technique is not perfect. In essence strong wind technique differs little from what you learnt as a beginner, but you need rather more strength and courage, and even a small mistake causes failure.

The main problems are raising the sail and keeping your balance before you get under way. It is quite hard to pull the sail out of the water because the strong wind thrusts it forcefully away from you. You have to use all your weight to pull it up, and when you have raised the rig far enough out of the water for the boom to emerge, pressure on the sail eases suddenly. If you are caught unawares you will fall back into the water and have to start the tedious business all over again. More skilful boardsailors therefore prefer the water start which requires considerably less strength, and I am going to describe that later. Be pre-

Important when winds are strong: the rig must be raked well to windward when getting under way.

After starting, hang your body out sideways and keep your arms almost straight.

The faster the board sails, the further aft can you stand on the board.

pared, then, for the moment when the boom leaves the water.

Raising the sail in a strong wind is much easier if you use the comfort rig described on p.95.

It is difficult to keep your balance now because the board is being tossed by the high waves which have been raised by the strong wind — at least in larger waters. But the weight of the rig will help you to balance if you let your sail hang to leeward with your arms outstretched, and the boom end just above the surface.

Get under way briskly so as to get pressure in the sail as soon as possible instead of trying to keep your footing without support.

You learnt how to start when you were a beginner, and the strong wind start is much the same. Raise the rig with the uphaul until the boom end is just out of the water and the sail slatting freely in the wind. Your foot positions are different; instead of your front foot being beside the mast it is just aft of the mast step while your back foot is just aft of the centreboard case.

Drop the uphaul and catch hold of the mast with your mast hand. You may possibly need to slip your back foot slightly further aft.

As you have already learnt, you now have to pull the rig past your body, directly towards the wind. Impress one thing on your mind: the stronger the wind, the further you have to pull your rig to windward. As you do this, your trunk turns towards the direction in which you will travel, and you will see the bow through the window in your sail. In a light wind you need to pull the sail far enough to windward for the boom to lie parallel to the water, but in a strong wind the boom end should point upwards.

Now catch hold of the boom with your sail hand, and pull it slightly towards you. When the board starts to make way you can harden in further and lean backwards. Do not be afraid of falling because you will be supported by the pressure on the sail. If the pull of the rig becomes too great, ease the sail out slightly with your sail hand.

When you find you can start like this in a hard wind without difficulty, you can take the next step. Pull the sail in vigorously, and simultaneously fall back to windward — the increased pressure on the sail will support your body.

Hardening the sail and dropping back in this way needs practice, and initially you will sometimes fall in because you drop back too far, or the rig will pull you over to leeward because you are too timid. As soon as your weight balances the wind pressure move your mast hand from the mast to the boom, and hook yourself on to your harness.

Beach start

When starting from the beach, you push the board into the water with the rig upright, which saves you the time-wasting business of raising the sail out of the water.

This is how the beach start goes; place your sailboard on the beach, rigged ready to sail, with the bow at the water's edge pointing offshore. Stand to windward holding the mast just above the boom with your mast hand. Your sail hand carries the board by a strap near the fin, which automatically tilts the board towards the mast.

Now push the board into the water, keeping it as nearly at right angles to the waves as possible; keep it close to you so as to prevent its being caught by a wave and swept sideways. It is important to keep the sail clear of the water.

When you reach the water that is roughly knee deep, watch the waves and drop the stern when a set of rather smaller waves approaches. Your sail hand is now free to grasp the boom. Immediately, move your front hand from the mast to the boom, but be careful to keep the angle of the board to the waves between 90° and 45°.

Wait for a suitable moment, for example after a set of waves has passed, and place your back foot on the board. Pressure on the sail is still slight because the rig is relatively low over the water, raked to windward.

Now harden the sail, which needs practice because the board tries to turn towards the wind. You prevent this by pushing on the boom to exert pressure on the mast and mast foot. Simultaneously pulling the board towards you with your back foot will help to discourage the board from luffing up when you don't want it to.

When the rig is lifted a little higher above the water, the increasing sail pressure will pull you onto the board. Do not step on to it deliberately, but let the sail *pull* you up onto it. As soon as your front foot is on the board, slip it immediately into the forward strap so that you can brace yourself and avoid a catapult fall.

The beach start is so easy. Hold the board by a footstrap and the mast, push it into knee-deep water, step on to it, and start.

The moment when you step up is the trickiest because there is no way on the board.

The shore at the water's edge should not be stony, or you will scratch or damaged the board or the fin. Short, light boards can be carried over stones and out into the water with your mast hand holding the boom and your sail hand in the strap furthest forward.

The nearer the direction of the wind is to directly offshore, the more difficult the beach start becomes, so make your first attempt when the wind is blowing slightly offshore or, best of all, parallel to the shore.

The water start

When sailing the dwarf among sailboards, the sinker, a waterstart is unavoidable, whereas with all other boards it is great fun. The water-start is one of the sophisticated refinements of boardsailing; it not only looks good but is quicker and saves energy.

However well you sail, strong wind is a must; with a wind of less than Force 4 a waterstart is impossible because pressure on the sail is insufficient. Only an exceptionally lightweight person can coax himself onto a board in a Force 3 wind.

There is one basic essential; you must have no fear of water, whether shallow or deep, because before you finally succeed you will be swimming

round for 10 or 20 minutes for sure, paddling and fussing round the board.

Spend enough time quietly in the water first, studying the way the board and rig react. Obviously you must be wearing a wet suit.

This is how it's done. As you lie in the water near the board and rig, check whether the rig is to windward with the boom end pointing to the stern. If not you have to turn either the board or the rig. This is rather troublesome with large boards, but chid's play with smaller ones. Sometimes you have to pull the mast over the stern; to do this, just prop yourself on the stern on one arm, and reach over to the mast lying in the water to leeward with the other,

and raise it slightly. The wind will lift the sail, and you can then easily pull the rig to windward over the stern above your head.

If the rig is already to windward but the boom end points towards the bow lift the mast top, work your way down the mast to the boom, and pull the rig towards the stern until the boom points to windward, then pull the boom

towards you, let it go suddenly and the wind will then swing it over to the right side. Now you are ready to try to get yourself pulled onto the board by the force of the wind in the sail.

Right, to start at the beginning, swim to the mast top and lift it slightly with one arm. A harness with buoyancy at the back is a help because it keeps your head above water.

The wind gets beneath the sail and lifts it, and as you work your way towards the board along the mast, gradually raising the rig higher, more wind gets into it. The water runs off aft, and will do so more easily if the boom is short. While you do this, try to swim backwards to windward so as to minimise leeway.

Work your way down until the boom

end is clear of the water, and try to keep the board at right angles to the wind; pulling the mast towards the wind direction will make it luff up, and wind force makes it bear away. The further forward the mast is stepped the easier this is.

When your mast hand reaches the level of the boom, catch hold of it with your sail hand. You should be right by the stern together with the rig. Now place your back foot on the board, and slip it into one of the stern straps, assuming there is one. You are now hanging from the rig, so to speak, and must put no weight whatsoever on your foot because if you do the board will luff up.

Finally, take hold of the boom with your mast hand, and at the same moment pull your back foot towards your body so as to make the board bear away. Your front leg will still be in the water, and you can make swimming movements with it to help the board to turn from a beam reach to a broad reach. As you do so, bring your centre of gravity, that is your bottom, as near to the board as possible.

The rig is now sufficiently upright

for the force of the wind to pull you up on to the board. You must really hang all your weight on the rig as it does so, and avoid pushing with your back foot because the board would then luff up when you don't want it to.

Allow your foot in the water to be drawn up onto the board, and slip it immediately into a footstrap so that you can brace yourself. Harden the sail right in, and straighten your trunk. You have made a successful waterstart!

The shorter the boom and the higher the clew, the easier it is to start from the water. It is not the size of the sail which matters, but its cut.

Practise in shallow water first so that you can stand on the bottom as you turn board and rig into the right position for starting; this saves the energy you would otherwise use swimming.

When sailing at speed, you do not stand on the board but hang from the boom.

Sailing at speed and planing

The main fascination for those who go in for strong wind sailing is speed. You suddenly start to tear along, the bow lifts and the board settles on the surface of the water, skipping over the waves with no increase in sail pressure. It's an exhilarating feeling, planing.

You hang beneath the boom with the water skimming past close beneath you, feeling as if you are floating on air. Perhaps it is because the elements are so extraordinarily close that planing at high speed so intoxicating. Experienced Funboard sailors reach speeds of 21 knots and more in Force 5 winds, while the current world record is over 30 knots. Experts even believe that 40 knots is within the realms of possibility. What a tremendous prospect.

A special technique is needed to get the most out of speed sailing, and this differs somewhat from what you have already learnt. You will remember that in light winds you stand on the board holding the rig in your hands, controlling it and steering with it. It is different now in Force 4 to 5 winds. Instead of standing on the board and holding the rig, you have to hang beneath the rig and transmit the power of the wind through your feet to the board. How can that be done?

Well, the stronger the wind, the further out to windward you must hang, so that your body weight counterbalances the wind pressure in

When planing, the sail is raked right aft but kept as upright as possible.

129

the sail. When the sail is raked to windward, wind force acts not only horizontally but upwards as well, just as is the case with an aeroplane wing. This upward acting force carries part of your weight; it is on this that you hang. When part of your body weight if offloaded from the board like this, the board will lift onto the surface of the water more readily, in other words, it will plane.

The secret of planing is therefore to reduce the weight on the board by hanging on the rig, and to lift the bow further and further out of the water by moving aft. You should not go too far aft, however, because then the stern will 'squat', and the drastic increase in the angle of attack of the board to the water brakes planing speed. One way to prevent squatting is to move your hands nearer the forward part of the boom so as to transmit force to the mast foot which, being well forward, will somewhat reduce the weight of your body on the stern. This technique of applying pressure to the mast food is used by many speed sailors, who can be seen standing in a somewhat hunched position, with their feet in the aftermost strap, hanging by their hands from the forward part of the boom.

In view of the relatively unsettled wind conditions that prevail in Britain and central Europe, it is a question of getting on the plane quickly and staying on it as long as possible. This means making the best use of the wind force that is available. Forward propulsion is greatest when the sail is as upright as is possible, because this keeps the component of wind force that acts upwards to the minimum while the component acting forwards is as great as it can be. However, less of your body's weight will be carried by the sail so you must transfer it to the mast foot, as just described.

One very important point is that the sail should be raked as far aft as the trim of the board allows, and that means that its foot will lie virtually on the deck. This discourages air from passing too easily beneath the foot from the high pressure area on the windward side of the sail to the low pressure zone on the lee side. The lower part of the sail will work more efficiently, which increases sail force, makes it easier to plane, and increases speed.

Once you are planing properly there is relatively little to do to increase speed. It is best to keep the board really flat on the water rather than pressing down the windward rail as many people do. You must also find the right angle of attack of the sail to the wind. The faster you sail, the stronger the wind that arises from the board speed and, therefore, the more you have to harden the sail. This means that when you are reaching at a high speed, your sail will be hardened in as far as if you were sailing closehauled at a much slower speed. Should you harden the sail in too far, laminar flow will separate, particularly near the leech, and cause turbulence which reduces speed.

You need to become sensitive so that you can combine all these speed-making factors. Sensitivity is certainly just as important as having a good sail, trimmed flat for speed, and a board with a good, smooth underwater surface.

Planing over the water, almost weightless, is the real delight of boardsailing. One dreams of repeating this fantastic experience over and over again.

Steering with your feet

As a beginner you learnt how to keep the sailboard at right angles to the wind while you raised the rig by putting more weight on one foot than on the other. You placed your feet either side of the centre of lateral resistance, and the board turned either to point closer to the wind or away from it, according to whether you put weight on to your back or your front foot.

The main difference between sailing an Allround board and planing on a Funboard is that, whereas with an Allround board all your weight is carried by the board, which you steer by raking the rig forward and aft, it is the Funboard's rig which carries all your weight while you steer with your feet. In light winds, you can only alter course by the 'shifting the position of the centre of effort relative to that of the centre of lateral resistance' principle, but by the time the wind is blowing at Force 4 there is the alternative of steering by immersing one of the rails

In strong winds, modern boards are no longer steered with the rig but by the feet.

instead of by altering the rake of the rig. It is essential to use your body correctly, because it is mainly on this that the new style of sailing depends.

You can only make use of the opportunities that Allround-Funboards offer in strong winds if you use footstraps, because you have to be in the right position on the board if you are to steer with your feet, and when the centre of gravity of your body is hanging so far out to windward, this is difficult without footstraps.

You steer with your feet either to alter course from sailing in a straight line or in order to initiate a tack or a power gybe. When sailing in surf, or even in the smaller wind-raised waves on inland waters, the real delight is that you can sail a slalom, turning and turning, without having to alter the rake of the rig, continuously using the thrust of a wave.

All you do when steering with your feet is to push or pull with them in the footstraps. Foot steering is only possible at higher speeds when dynamic lift is considerable because it is the braking effect when pressure is applied to the weather or lee rail which causes the board to curve round, just as happens with a water ski or a surfboard.

It is the development of this technique that has led to the new style of boardsailing, which calls for winds of at least Force 4.

Gradually bring your front foot further aft, without altering the rake of the sail. Should the board luff up, transfer more weight forward and harden the sail in slightly. This will transfer some of your body weight on to the mast foot, which is forward of the centre of lateral resistance. Now alter course very quickly; to bear away bend both knees so as to transfer more weight forward, but to luff up straighten your legs to transfer weight aft. As well as shifting your weight forward or aft, you move it laterally to immerse one of the rails at the stern; this is a very important element of steering.

In surf, in particular, you need to be able to alter course quickly and correctly when sailing in high waves. At first, try to luff or bear away only slightly by putting weight on the rails with your back foot. Once you feel more confident, you can turn more sharply and make better use of your sail. Finally you will be able to swing right into a tack or gybe.

Applying pressure on the lee rail makes the board bear away immediately, as is required for a power gybe.

The power gybe

Gybing worries many boardsailors. They simply do not trust themselves to change tack with the wind aft. One reason must be that it is not as easy to gype an Allround board as to go about. Another is surely prejudice because, in sailing boats, gybing is tricky and can be dangerous. Lack of gybing practice means that the boardsailor is not adept. However it is easier to gybe a modern Allround-Funboard or a Funboard than to put it about, provided that you practise enough.

The advantage of a cleanly executed gybe is that, whereas the board comes almost to a standstill when tacking, it does not lose way while gybing, and the stability which results from dynamic lift is therefore maintained. Secondly, when gybing, the period when there is no pressure on the sail is much shorter than when tacking, and that means there is a smaller chance of losing one's balance. Thirdly, your body turns through only 90° when you gybe, as against 260° while you are tacking, and this again means that you will be less stable when tacking. Fourthly, if a board is under 3m long, the mast foot is often so far forward that the bow will nose dive when the board is put about.

This is how to do a quick power gybe: use your feet to make the board bear away; when on the run, gybe the sail, harden in, and plane away again on the other tack.

There are a number of different ways of gybing; you can turn really tightly, but that means applying considerable pressure at the stern which will slow the board markedly, whereas sailing a much wider curve and using a power gybe enables you to maintain board speed as you alter course. The first method is particularly suitable for very short boards when you want to change tack without dropping too far to leeward, while the second gybe is the answer when you turn to sail offshore again after riding a wave.

The vital factor for a power gybe is to steer properly with your feet. You can see how to do this in the series of photographs.

You are surfing at high speed on a beam reach, with your feet still in the footstraps. Unhook yourself from the harness line, and check that the water will be clear when you gybe.

Keep the rig hardened in and upright, slip your front foot into the aftermost of the forward straps, and put your back foot close to whichever rail will be on the inside of the turn.

Bear away by applying pressure to the inside rail with your back foot, and bend your knee as you do so. Your front foot helps to immerse the inside rail by lifting the outside one. Keep the rig upright and hardened in.

You are now almost on a run, your speed is reduced, and you ease out the sail.

Now exchange the positions of your feet; move your back foot quite far forward, and slip your front foot out of the strap and back to the stern.

Continue to keep weight on the inside rail so that the board carries on turning, and pull the mask back towards the stern until the boom is pointing forward at an angle. The board luffs up, and pressure on the sail increases.

It is time to gybe the rig. Your sail hand releases the boom and, after the sail has swung round, grabs hold of the mast beneath the boom and pulls the rig to windward again.

With what was your mast hand, catch hold of the boom as rapidly as possible, and harden in the sail. Slip your back foot into a footstrap quickly so as to avoid being whipped off to windward.

Sail pressure eases now, and your speed increases again. Pull the mast back with a jerk, and catch hold of the boom with your mast hand.

This completes the gybe, and you can now hook complete onto the harness line again, sailing on with your feet in the appropriate footstraps.

The quick tack

The first manoeuvre that a beginner learns is to tack, and he generally becomes adept relatively quickly. However, it is advisable to practise the jump tack, which is suitable for every type of board, not just Funboards, so as to be absolutely certain and to be able to tack really quickly. . .

It is actually easier to tack Allround-Funboards because they are relatively more stable, and it is preferable to change tack by going about rather than by gybing because you will drop considerably less far to leeward when you tack. It is a great deal trickier with smaller boards which often have no centreboards; gybing is the answer for them.

But why the term 'quick' tack

anyway? There is only one permanent force available to the Funboard sailor; he can rely only on the rig, which he himself controls. It is therefore important that he should keep the time when there is no pressure on the sail to the minimum. It is not the whole process of going about that has to be quick, just the critical phase when the sail is slatting empty of wind; that is what must be kept as brief as possible.

This is how to do a quick tack out on the water.

You start planing on a beam reach with your feet in the footstraps. Unhook yourself from the harness line with a short sharp pull on the boom. Immediately afterwards move your mast hand from the boom to the mast,

The quick tack is used only when longer boards are beating, and in races. Luff up, applying some weight to the rail, and jump onto the other side; when the board is head to wind, throw the mast forward and to windward with your mast hand, sheet in and plane away.

keeping your mast arm straight and your sail arm bent so that the sail is still close hauled. You will automatically crouch slightly as you do this.

Now to luff up. You rake the rig aft until the boom end is just above the water. Again a high clew sail is preferable because the boom end must not dip into the water. Encourage the bow to turn towards the wind by putting weight on the weather rail.

Take your feet out of the straps and move near the mast foot. Pull the clew of the sail back to windward of the centreline in order to accelerate the turning motion. You are standing quite upright now, and can apply pressure with your back foot to help the board to turn.

Now comes the tricky moment when the board is bow to wind and making no way; you must be quick. You jump round the mast and, at the same time, your sail hand grabs the mast and pulls the rig forward. You have to jump and change hands at lightening speed to avoid an involuntary swim because this is the unstable phase when there is no pressure on the sail to steady you.

After jumping round, place your front foot just ahead of the mast foot, and your back foot relatively far aft. Now rake the rig further forward and simultaneously to windward.

Although there is still no pressure in the sail, you must nevertheless be prepared for the fact that you will have to

hang out to windward as soon as you sheet in the sail.

With your new sail hand gripping the boom, and your mast hand keeping hold of the mast while you harden in, you thrust with your front foot to help the board bear away. You will only succeed in doing this if you have raked the rig far enough forward and to windward.

Slip your back foot into a footstrap now because the increasing pressure in the sail as the board gathers way could pull you over to leeward. Lean back to windward, but keep hold of the mast with your front hand because that will automatically rake the rig further forward, and you will be able to bear away further.

Once you are on your new course, move your front foot from its position by the mast back to one of the footstraps, and then shift your mast hand to the boom. You are then back in your normal sailing position, having completed your fast tack.

Body dip and head dip

There are countless variations to the games that can be played with the wind and waves when it is blowing hard, and among them are body dip and head dip.

For *body dip* you pull the mast right over to windward and throw yourself back against the wind until your body touches the water, and is enveloped in a rising cloud of spray. Then you speed close above the water in a scorching plane. As you will realise, body dip is not for those who are afraid of the water.

When you are sailing fast on a beam reach, bend your knees and hang right under the boom with your backside fairly close to the rail and just above the water. This brings your centre of gravity very low. When wind pressure increases, stretch your legs without bending your arms. Try now to lower your body until it actually touches the water, and then sheet in the sail slightly with your sheet hand so that the increased pressure in the sail will lift you onto the board again.

For *head dip* you only submerge

A wet boardsailing game, played for sheer fun: the only real uses of head dip and body dip are to cool down after a hectic ride.

your head, not your whole body. Just as for body dip you sail on a beam reach in a Force 4-5 wind, leaning well out to windward. Instead of lowering your body until it is close to the water, you hollow your back as much as you can and drop your head back. You can see the world behind you upside down — an extraordinary feeling at high speed. If you now bend your knees slightly, your body will arch downwards and your head will just touch the water.

In waves, your head will be more deeply submerged, of course, and for a short while you will not be able to see. Nor can you watch your sail, and that means that you will not be able to control it so well.

Head dip gives you a really impressive view if you open your eyes as you dip your head.

Strong wind falls

No strong wind boardsailor can escape full-blooded falls. We are not talking now about those gentle flops into the water that are part of every learner's repertoire in the early stages, but of falls such as capsize and catapult falls that can be anticipated but are nevertheless unavoidable.

When sailing in strong winds there are moments — and you will recognise them clearly, for example as you bear away — when the boom drags you forward forcibly and your back foot is lifted off the board even though you are using your last ounce of strength trying to stand firm. You know then that, a fraction of a second later, you will be catapulted through the air, and the mast will crash down with fearful force onto the deck or into the water.

The catapult fall, rarely intentional, often unavoidable, but very spectacular for those watching.

Catapult fall

This is undoubtedly one of the most gymnastic ways of leaving your board. It often occurs when you want to bear away to sail at maximum speed, just after you get under way. Wind pressure on the sail increases, and the centre of effort moves higher up the sail. The result is that you can no longer counter the extra pressure of the wind on the sail by strength and body weight alone, the rig crashes forward at an angle with enormous force and all you can do is to fly after it.

The best method of trying to avoid this when bearing away is to rake your mast not only forward but also to windward so that you can use your body weight more effectively. Concentrate, and be deliberate in your actions. If you feel the pull on your sail is excessive, ease it out slightly but be sure to keep the rig rake well to windward. Keeping your back foot in a footstrap will make it easier for you to brace yourself, and that will help you to stay with the board.

Capsize fall

Have you ever experienced this? You have worked some way to windward and are looking forward to an exciting broad reach back. You get going, but not for long because one of the board's rails lifts up suddenly and irresistably and whips you right over — that is a capsize fall.

This is caused by the centreboard because waterflow differs on either side of it due to leeway; the water

streams past at a very small angle to the board, which means that pressure is lower on one side, and that causes suction. The faster the board sails, the greater the suction, and the more forcibly will the centreboard try to lift towards the surface of the water.

The rule is that the smaller the centreboard, the smaller the forces that can act on it. This is why a retractable centreboard has to be stowed away within the hull when you are on a fast point of sailing.

Diving fall

The name gives the clue to this fall, which is particularly likely to happen when you are reaching or running. The forward part of the board cuts beneath the water's surface and goes on diving. Once it has dived deep enough it will probably suddenly shoot sideways and upwards, and you will generally be thrown into the water. This is particularly common with boards that have little or no scoop.

When sailing fast down into a wave trough, move both feet aft to lift the board's nose clear at the critical point — the back of the wave ahead.

Dangers in strong winds

Generally speaking there are few dangers when boardsailing inland, provided you are a reasonably good swimmer and know the right of way rules. Apart from spectacular falls, there is little that can go wrong; after all, you only fall into water.

When sailing inland and the wind freshens to such an extent that you cannot support the rig any longer, you can stand and hold the rig by the uphaul, and let yourself be driven to a nearby bank with the sail flapping. You can trail the end of the boom lightly in the water, and the wind will then fill a small portion of the sail. This will give you headway with the wind abeam, but you will move slowly.

A more experienced boardsailor can also reduce the area of the sail by reefing when the wind is extremely strong. Just release the downhaul and push the lower part of the sail up to the boom, where you make the downhaul fast to the boom fitting. This reduces the area of the sail by the amount of the triangle beneath the boom. Be careful not to pull the mast out of the mast foot when you are pushing the sail up.

Should you be unable to reach a nearby bank using these methods, you have no alternative but to make the international distress signal (waving your arms up and down). Never panic in such a situation and, whatever you do, stay on your board because you know it is unsinkable and therefore the ideal life float.

The dangers are much greater off the coast. Sailing in strong wind can rapidly become a disaster if, for example, some part of the board breaks when the wind is blowing off the land. You will then be driven helplessly out to sea, and will be in extreme danger if no-one on land has been keeping an eye on you. This is why you should take a few life-saving rules to heart.

● Do not boardsail in a strong offshore wind.

● Find out from local inhabitants or the coastguard the characteristics of the coastal areas, ie tides, currents, sandbanks, wrecks, shipping lanes etc.

● Always wear a wet suit when boardsailing in strong winds at sea because of the great danger of hypothermia. You will become colder in a strong wind on a hot day than when the wind is light and the air cold.

● The most important rule is that your rig must be connected to the board with a leash. If you are catapulted off, the mast foot could easily be released, and it is seldom possible to catch up with the board by swimming because it is driven downwind too fast when the wind is strong. The safety leash should lead from the mast to the towing eye at the nose, so that the board will lie bow to wind and therefore drift more slowly to leeward.

● Always carry a spare line with you — if not in a rucksack, lash it round the the end of the boom.

● Check every detail of your board thoroughly before setting out in strong winds, so that you can be really sure that nothing will break when you are out on the water.

Sailing technique for experts

Modern boards sail so fast that you can even jump with the help of the small waves which form on inland waters.

Jumping in smooth water

For a long time, only surf specialists were able to jump high out of the water into the air, but the breakthrough came with the planing boards which are fast and, most important of all, really light weight; they can take off with the help of the mini waves that form of inland waters, and fly briefly through the air.

Your equipment must be appropriate if you are able to jump relatively easily. Less energy is required to accelerate a board weighing less than 18kg, with a broad flat planing bottom. Your mast should be light too, but stiff so that you can control your sail more easily and precisely. Admittedly a

softer mast is pleasanter to use because it will absorb the shock better when the board thumps down hard on the waves, but anyone whose main interest is jumping in smooth waters should go for a hard mast.

The sail must be neither too limp nor too heavy. The rig described on p. 96 has proved very satisfactory at the higher speeds which make jumping possible.

The area

What sort of area is needed if you intend to try jumping for the first time? Because the absolute minimum wind strength required is Force 4, and Force 5-6 is obviously better because the waves which act as your springboard are higher too, you need to establish where the wind is blowing hardest. That will usually be on the lee side of a lake; the wind is also less gusty there, and the waves will be higher than on the weather side. Search out a patch where the waves are deflected from the wind direction; this will generally be where a tongue of land projects into the water. Keep a look out, too, for cross waves, which are waves superimposed on the normal pattern.

They come from a completely different direction, usually as a result of a wind shift, and are ideal springboards. You need to be patient and to use your eyes before you learn to pick them out so that you can make the best use of them.

Technique

Sail as fast as you can and as close to the wind as you can. With a planing board, that will generally mean a beam reach because you slow down if you point any closer to the wind.

In surf, most of the energy which lifts you into the air comes from the force of the waves, but inland it is your own strength, used at exactly the right instant to thrust the board off the wave, that will lift the board. Technique is therefore all-important. You make the board jump out of the

While in the air you have to lift the weather rail so as to avoid diving down nose first.

water by straightening both legs quickly, simultaneously forcing down the lee rail and sheeting in the sail.

Pressure on the lee rail reduces leeway and enables you to point higher so that you can approach the wave at a more acute angle; it also increases lift, and helps the board to rise higher from the water.

The moment you take off is immediately after the moment when wave thrust is greatest, and you will at once be aware of the instant reduction in the pressure on your feet. In order to jump vertically, keep your legs straight and force yourself and the board back, but if you want the board to fly through the air horizontally, bend your knees momentarily. You need to land on the water on a beam reach, so raise the weather rail and push the lee rail down; the board will then bear away in the air. Whatever you do, do not thrust the weather rail down because a fall is the virtually inevitable consequence.

Shortly before you touch down, bend your knees slightly to absorb the shock. While you are in the air, keep the sail sheeted in to ensure that its aerodynamic efficiency is maintained.

All this takes but a few seconds of course but even if you have only lifted the board a few centimetres out of the water you will be so delighted that you will want to start getting ready for another attempt straight away.

The duck gybe

The duck gybe is a variation of the power gybe, the major difference being that, instead of swinging the rig round with the clew passing over the bow, you duck under the foot of the sail while the clew passes over the stern.

The whole sequence of turning movements is reversed; whereas with a power gybe you start by turning the board onto the new course with your feet and only gybe the sail afterwards, with a duck gybe you swing the rig over before or at the same moment as altering course with your feet. You need to be on the plane when starting a duck gybe, because it is only when you are sailing very fast that you can duck under the boom, grab hold of the opposite side and then harden the rig right in immediately.

The best moment to duck gybe is when you are sailing on the face of a wave, because then the board will not slow down, even when there is no pressure in the sail, and it may even accelerate. This gives you plenty of time to put board and rig onto the opposite gybe.

When waves are of only of medium size and you cannot ride them properly, the duck gybe is not suitable because the stern often slips sideways while you are gybing.

There are many different variations of this gybe. Some depend on the type of board; with a sinker, for example, your gybe can be very tight because you - turn board and rig virtually simultaneously. On a long racing Funboard, however, you gybe the rig very early before you even start to use your feet to change course.

The following series of photographs shows how to do it. First bear away to sail at maximum speed so as to reduce the relative wind to the minimum during the next few seconds. Move your sail hand further back than its normal position, and shift your back foot from the footstrap to the lee rail.

Tilt the board further. With your mast hand catch hold of the boom close by your sail hand, whether just forward or just aft of it. The mast will swing down to leeward at this instant. There will be almost no pressure in the sail due to your high speed.

Your sail hand lets go, and the mast swings further forward. This transfers the whole weight of the rig through the mast foot to the board, and accelerates the turn. Still keep the board tilted to help it turn sharply.

Now duck slightly and the foot of the sail will swing over your head. You have borne away so far that there is no pressure in the sail, and that allows you to pull the rig aft with your former mast hand while your new mast hand catches hold of the boom forward of the centre of effort.

As soon as your mast hand has grasped the boom on what is now the windward side, let go of the lee side of it with your other hand and catch hold of the weather boom near the clew to ease the rig out slightly, otherwise your sail would be sheeted in too far for when you start to luff.

Only now, when luffing up, do you change the position of your feet. Your back foot which was on the lee rail (now the weather rail) is moved forward and slipped into a strap while what was your forward foot moves aft.

The whole gybe lasts less than three seconds and looks like child's play to an observer. It is worth practising the duck gybe because you will enjoy doing it.

Boardsailing in surf

Surf-sailing must be the most exciting boardsailing experience. The power of the mighty waves of the open sea becomes visible when it is unleashed as the waves roll in in apparently unending succession to explode onto the beach with fearsome force. It seems impossible that a human being could survive such power with so fragile a craft.

The attraction of surf-sailing is not just the danger. It is far more a case of the thrill of speed when a fast-moving wave rushes the boardsailor along with it, and the excitement of manoeuvring skilfully on the face of a wave. Above all there is the challenge of swinging through these restless mountains, picking one's way in surroundings which are themselves changing continuously, where every instant there is a different situation to resolve. You become more and more skilful, but there are always more difficult variations to face, and consequently new satisfactions to enjoy.

Quite apart from reliable gear, sure boardsailing technique and physical fitness, you need courage and quick reactions. You also need to know something of the dynamics of water in surf. Given proper caution, the right gear and considerable practise, every advanced boardsailor can try his surfing skill in waves one or two metres, 3-6ft, high.

*When riding a wave, surf-sailing involves
two basic manoeuvres; the Bottom Turn in
the wave trough, when you sail a long
curve away from the wind. After sailing up
the wave face again you turn sharply at
the lip, and the Cut Back takes you down
to the trough again.*

151

The area

First attempts should not be made in heavy surf. It is far better to try in light surf to start with, with a rather stronger wind blowing nearly parallel to the shore. A sandy beach or bay is essential so that you have a soft landing when the inevitable occurs.

Waves

What causes waves anyway? When wind blows over the surface of water, friction causes roughness which, due to the continuing pressure on the water molecules, moves forward as waves. The harder and longer that the wind blows from one direction, and the greater the distance over open water which it has blown, the higher the waves.

It is not the height of a wave, measured from crest to trough, that indicates its severity, but height related to wave length, measured between successive crests. The shorter the length the more awkward the wave. A 4m (12ft) high wave, for example, is much more difficult to deal with in the Baltic, where its length will be about 90 feet, than a wave of the same height in the North Sea with a length of 60-70m (190-220ft). When the wind drops, the waves which persist for some while are called swell.

Surf waves differ from shore to shore Before setting out, you have to observe their patterns closely and check on currents.

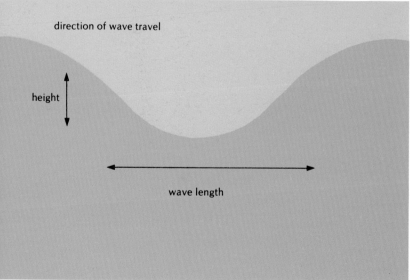

Waves are formed as a result of continuous pressure. The water particles only move in a circle from top to bottom.

direction of wave travel

height

wave length

Waves do not build up to great heights in the open sea because much of the accumulated energy is dissipated continuously when they break. The mass of water only appears to move forward. In reality it is just the shape of the surface of the sea that alters unceasingly as the water rises at the crests and falls in the troughs. A floating object stays in the same place, moving up and down endlessly and, at most, may be blown slightly downwind.

When consideraing the deep sea, it is only the surface of the water that is disturbed to form waves. Where there are shoals and banks, and near the shore, the sea becomes shallower and the water particles, which follow a circular path in the deeper water, cannot swing down in a full circle. The rising sea bed forces the water upwards, causing the waves to break as surf thundering on the shore. Where there are off-lying sandbanks, the waves rolling in break as surf much further offshore.

A 4m (13ft) high breaker will hurl between 20 and 50 tons of water forward onto a beach close by a board-sailor and, whereas the water in the ocean waves only appears to advance, the white streaks and patches of foam in the surf show how extremely fast the water actually moves near the shore. It runs far up the beach before sweeping back to the sea, often as undertow beneath the next incoming wave. This undercurrent can be strong and clutching, and has been fatal to many swimmers, especially where beaches are wide and flat. It can even drag you out when you are standing in hip deep water.

Tides and currents

There is a special challenge to surf-sailing in areas where the tide ebbs and flows and it can be dangerous. Regardless of wind direction, in many areas the tidal streams set along the coast, first in one direction and then in the opposite direction, at a speed varying from hour to hour and from locality to locality. In some tidal waters the speed at which the tidal stream sets is negligible but in others it sets too fast to be ignored. It is therefore essential to find out about local tidal streams before setting out

and, once you are out on the water, to check regularly to see how you are being set in relation to a landmark on shore such as a house, trees, an oddly shaped sand dune or rocks. Swimming gear left on the beach is invisible when you are offshore.

Never underestimate the effects of tidal streams and local peculiarities. In some river and harbour entrances, where enormous masses of water force their way through a narrow passage, the water can run up to six knots. If the wind is blowing in the same direction as the tidal stream is setting it may well be impossible to gain distance to windward, however skilful you are. Another problem is that wind blowing against a current causes the waves to become steeper and to break. Wind with a current smoothes out the waves. The former type of sea may be very difficult to sail through, though the current will at least carry you to windward.

The water is rough off seaward-facing beaches affected by tides. During the flood tide the surf becomes steeper and, where there are offlying banks or shoals and where the sea bed is uneven, it may be so chaotic that it is very difficult or impossible to work out beyond the zone of breakers. Strong undertows and eddies occur during the ebb in the area of fast-moving streaks of foam. But apart from occasions when there is a dead offshore wind, boardsailors will find delightful surf, resulting from seas rolling in un-interruptedly from a great distance, along these offshore facing beaches.

The water off the inland-facing shores, for example off islands, is calmer and disturbed only by wind-raised seas but be careful, the tidal streams are almost always very strong, especially in the narrows between islands.

Starting in surf

Before setting out, check the following points carefully:

● Are there stones, stakes, offlying sandbanks or similar obstructions?
● Is there a quieter area where the waves barely break?
● How often do the extra large waves roll in?
● At what frequency are sets of larger waves followed by sets of smaller waves?

These are the factors which determine the right place at which to start, and the right moment in relation to the rhythm of the surf.

Watch for a while so that you become acquainted with the characteristics of the area.

Timing is all-important because you need to use the opportunities that present themselves; that means making a mental note of when and where a wave will break, how high it is and how much force it has. Then again, is it rolling in alone or advancing with a set, because a set of lower waves is followed by several higher ones.

When starting, you have to search for the right wave by waiting for a quiet moment, possibly between two sets, and only then do you jump on the board to set off. Your timing has to be right so that you do not reach the next wave just when it is breaking; you have to regulate your speed as you approach it.

Many methods of starting have been tried out, but the beach start has proved to be both the fastest and the

Before setting out, observe the surf really carefully and work out how you can save yourself should your equipment be damaged.

Wait in knee-deep water until a break in the waves makes it possible for you to sail out to sea.

After the wave has passed, jump on the board and use the suction of the returning wave to pull you out to sea.

surest. You have already learnt the basics of the beach start, but there are some points particularly worth noting. If the wind is blowing from the right, hold your board near the fin with your left hand while your right grips the mast. When the wind is blowing from your left, your right hand holds the board and your left the mast. You must always be to windward and the board to leeward. Try to keep the board at right angles to the wind all the time so as to prevent it from being whipped sideways and capsized.

With the wind blowing roughy parallel to the waves, and having pushed your board into the water and let it fall, you must stay close by it, holding it by the boom. Standing like this, you can control the board by pushing or pulling on the boom while you wait for the right moment to set out. The water must be deep enough for you to jump on the board, so you will have to take two or three steps offshore with it, and that will give you

sufficient way to sail over the first incoming wave.

Practise this modified beach start on inland waters first. If you find that you fail after your fourth or fifth attempt, you can be sure that you would do no better offshore in the conditions that prevail there.

If you fail to get started, pull all your equipment out of the water as quickly as you can, because the breaking waves are dangerous and can cause sails to be torn or mast and boom broken. The danger of being injured is also quite high, so you must take care; never let the board get between you and the next wave because the force of the wave can sometimes throw a board several metres high. Be prepared to jump clear of the danger area if you have to.

Another tip is to refuse help when learning to start because if your own strength and skill are not up to it when you try to start from the beach you will be sure to fail when your try offshore.

Sailing out against the waves

Once you have managed to start, slip your feet into the footstraps and quickly try to gather speed so that you can work your way out through the breakers without difficulty. Again it is a question of observation and timing. Where are the approaching waves smallest? And where are they breaking least?

As the wave approaches, you start by bearing away and sailing towards it at an obtuse angle, no smaller than

45°. When you reach your chosen spot and the wave is only a few metres away, luff up slightly and shift your weight well aft to lift the bow so that the wave can run beneath the board. You bear away again immediately afterwards to get up enough speed for the following wave when you repeat the exercise. If you are doubtful whether you can sail over the wave, you can always bear away, gybe before it reaches you, and ride it shorewards where you can tack and start out again.

If you shift your weight to the stern just before a breaking crest reaches you, you will prevent the board from burying its bow beneath the surface.

Wave riding

The great excitment of surfing is wave-riding. Your speed when sailing in on surf is due not only to wind force but to the speed at which the wave itself is moving.

Yet again timing is vital if you are to ride the face of a wave correctly.

Starting on the face is called Take Off. You start when the wave has almost reached the board, and sheet the sail in quickly so as to accelerate. If your timing is wrong, either because the wave was faster or because you started late and were not sailing fast enough to stay on the face, the wave will just run past beneath the board.

After take off you surf down the wave, sailing at an angle down the face to make maximum use of the thrust of the wave. At times your speed will be extremely high and, although it cannot be measured, it may well exceed the fastest speeds achieved so far in record attempts.

When you reach the foot of the wave, you can either sail away from it or let yourself be carried up to its crest in a long drawn out curve to leeward. Accelerate as much as you can as you bear away, because your speed will drop as you sail up the face again. The bottom turn, which you initiate by forcing the lee rail down, is the first part of an S curve which is completed at the crest. When you reach the crest, luff up vigorously by weighting the weather rail and tilting the board sharply. This manoeuvre, called Off the Lip or Cut Back, shoots you down the face of the wave again and you then start to make your way to the crest with another bottom turn.

You should swing up and down like this at the critical part of the wave of course, in other words where it is steepest. The best ways is to search for the place where a row of waves starts to break before you even set off. If you then sail down the face of your wave just ahead of the white water your curve to leeward will bring you back to the steepest part.

You need a great deal of experience, of course, plus a good eye and the ability to react quickly, when you play this thrilling game amongst the wandering sea mountains. But your sense of achievement is greatest of all in surf where your ability is tested to the utmost.

Swinging on the face of a wave is rather like skiing in deep snow, except that you leave no tracks. Sailing in surf can never become boring because every day is different — and so is every wave.

Jumping in surf

Jumping in surf is a game for experts. It is not only in Hawaii that you can take to the air for a short flight; sailboards can be catapulted over the waves wherever there is surf. The essential is that the wind should not blow from the same direction as that in which the waves are travelling but at right angles to them or slightly offshore. The higher the waves the less strong need the wind be. In such conditions jumping goes something like this.

Observation

After starting from the beach you sail out on a beam or broad reach, watching the sets and discovering where the waves break. Once you have selected your 'springboard', ease out the sail so that you can regulate your speed as you approach the wave. Should it break too soon sheet in the sail and let the foam crest pass beneath the board. Never just steer blindly towards a wave.

The approach

Place your feet as far apart as you can in footstraps that are relatively far aft so that you can control the board properly with your feet.

Two factors now combine; the board's own speed and the speed of the approaching wave. Together they provide sufficient speed for you to take to the air.

The essential now is to sail towards the wave at the correct angle on the correct point of sailing. You will generally sail too slowly if you are close hauled or on a beam reach at right angles to the wave, and you will not then be able to jump either far or high. If you approach the wave at an acute angle on a beam reach you will jump further rather than higher, with the board flying roughly horizontal through the air. On the other hand, if you sail at right angles to the wave on a broad or beam reach the board will shoot high in the air when you jump, but will not move forward.

Timing is vital: you must jump at just the right moment, having reached the wave a fraction of a second before it breaks.

The jump

Once you are on the wave face, sheet the sail right in and luff up slightly. Then thrust the lee rail down as hard as you can and, with your foot in the strap, pull the weather rail up towards you. Only the stern will be in contact with the crest now; the bow is already in the air.

One tip which will help you jump successfully is this: force the lee rail down hard just before lift off, because the wind will then get beneath the weather rail and this helps to lift the board.

162

Timing is vital when you jump in breaking surf. If you catch the wave before it breaks you will fly some distance through the air, but if you take off where it is steepest you will jump high.
Below: an Upside Down jump; the mast tip will often touch the water.

In the air

Once the stern has left the wave, you will know roughly at what angle your board is lying in the air. If the bow is pointing upwards steeply and you feel you will drop onto your back, you have to pull the board towards your body, against the pull of the rig, by bending your arms and legs. On the other hand if your stern is rather too high and you anticipate diving into the water nose first, you have to stretch your arms and legs to force the stern down.

Broadly speaking, when you want to jump high you pull the rig firmly towards you and simultaneously throw yourself backwards. The board will then stand nearly on end, and the sail above you will act like an aerofoil. When jumping forward, draw your legs up slightly to keep the board roughly horizontal. You will then lose little forward speed and fly a good deal further.

It is important to make the board bear away during the flying phase, and to avoid luffing up. It will bear away automatically if you force the lee rail down when you take off.

Jumping in surf is not as dangerous as it looks. All that happens is that you fall into water.

Landing

Flying through the air is exhilarating, but all too soon the rude awakening of landing comes — a hard thump down which you have to absorb with your knees. The stern of the sailboard should land first, flat, not tilted. On no account land with your knees straight.

The higher you have jumped the greater will be the reduction in your forward speed. You must therefore ease the sail out as you land because, if you touch down with the sail full, the wind will immediately whip you off the board to leeward. You sheet in again afterwards to get sailing again.

The whole sequence of movements takes less than a couple of seconds. Even a long, high jump takes little longer. This is why it is so important to react instantly and to be in full control. If you feel the board is getting away

from you and you anticipate falling, slip your feet out of the footstraps, push yourself away from the flying board, and simultaneously throw the boom down to leeward.

It is important to bear the following points in mind when jumping:

● Your footstraps must fit your feet properly (see p. 107). If they are too roomy, your whole foot could slip through when the shock of landing comes, and that could endanger your life. If the straps are too tight, your feet will slip out while you are in the air, and the board will then drop down beneath your feet.
● Choose a board with a narrow bow for extreme wind and wave conditions.
● Always check the area carefully at low water when you can see any rocks or reefs on which you could injure yourself.
● When falling, do not dive in head first but push yourself clear of rig and board with your hands and feet.
● When you surface after a fall, protect your head with your arms in case something which could land on you is still falling.
● Every time you are about to jump, check carefully that nobody is swimming or engaged in some other form of water sport in the area where you will land.

Safety — rules

Undisputedly, the principle on which every boardsailor should operate when sailing in surf is — safety first. If you heed the following points which relate to your own safety and that of others, you are not likely to get into difficulties.

● Never go out alone in surf. If you have no companion with you, at the very least inform someone on shore. Tell someone of your plans if you intend to make a longer trip, and give a rough idea of the time you expect to be back.
● Every time you set out, find out first what wind and weather conditions to expect, whether there are local signs of changes in the weather (such as rain or fog), and details of the tidal streams and current in the area.
● Study the shore carefully. Where can you land in a hurry if need be, and where would it be unsafe? Are there reefs and rocks hidden under water, or shallow areas such as sandbanks? Where do people swim?
● Shortly before setting out, watch the waves closely. Try to establish the rhythm of the waves, and check to find which way they are moving.
● Do not decide that you can manage without a wet suit because the wind is light; when learning to surf-sail you will often finish up in the water, and evaporation lowers body temperature very rapidly.
● Check that the mast foot fits firmly into the mast step. It must not jump out every time you sail over a wave.
● You must take a spare line about 1.50m long on the boom or in your harness' rucksack so that you have a replacement downhaul or outhaul.

● The rig must be connected to the sailboard by a leash, which must lead from the mast foot to the bow so that the board will lie at right angles to the breakers after a fall, not across them.
● If your rig is damaged or carried away, stay with your board and paddle it as far as the zone of breakers; there it will become a dangerous projectile so you have to jump in and swim the rest of the way to the shore. Always aim for the safest place to land rather than the nearest.
● Should you lose your board offshore, swim to the land with the help of the waves. Never take off your wet suit, even if you feel hampered by it, because it provides extra buoyancy as well as stopping you getting cold so quickly.

As to other sportsmen nearby:

● Surfers often wait offshore a very long time for the right wave. Keep your distance and avoid the zone where they are surfing.
● The official right of way rules are not appropriate vis-a-vis other boardsailors when sailing surf. As a general rule, give way to everybody in so far as conditions allow you to do so.
● There is one unwritten rule: someone working out to sea gives way to someone coming in. The latter is making full use of the thrust of the wave he is riding, and is very restricted in his ability to manoeuvre, whereas the man sailing out to sea can more easily sheet out his sail and slow down to let the other man past.

Whatever the emergency, the golden rule is:
Stay calm, keep a clear head so that you can review the situation, and quietly take whatever steps are needed to initiate rescue from the shore. The man who panics aggravates the situation!

Freestyle
boardsailing

It started in America, like everything else, where the Californian and Hawaiian coast boardsailors got tired of sailing normally all the time. They wanted to be able to do more, to improve control of their boards and to open up new dimensions for their sport. This led to freestyle. Performing tricks effortlessly, especially on the larger boards, gave pleasure and a feeling of achievement, even in light winds.

Enthusiasm spread from the USA to Europe where more and more freestyle competitions are now held each year. The object is to perform as many different tricks as possible and, as with ice skating, to assemble them into a programme. A jury then decides how many points to award to each competitor.

Freestyle is not restricted to competitions of course, and is most fun when done just for show without being under pressure. Do not run away with the idea that such tricks are only for sailboard acrobats. Some of them are so easy that any relatively able boardsailor can master them with a little practice. A number of the best-known tricks performed today are described here, but do not let this limit your own inventiveness and so, work out your own new variations. A routine will usually include fast and jet tacks, running and stop gybes, body dip, head dip and water starts, all of which are skills that the keen strong wind boardsailor will have learnt anyway. But now some of the special freestyle tricks.

Rail-riding

The best boardsailing trick is to sail the board deliberately on its side, a trick invented by World Champion Robby Naish. You force the lee side of the board under the water and pull the windward rail up with your other foot. You can then stand or sit right on the edge, balancing by pulling the sail towards you. Real experts can ride the leeward rail too, rail side backwards and tack or gybe on the rail.

Helicopter or 360° turn

This starts with a stop gybe when you back the sail against the wind. Keep pushing and follow the sail round until the entire rig has turned a circle. Now sheet in and get under way again.

Sailing to leeward

This is exactly opposite to your normal way of sailing. Instead of pulling the sail towards you and to windward you stand on the lee side of the board and push the rig towards the wind. You can do this facing the sail or, as the experts prefer, lean back negligently against the boom to counter the pressure of the wind.

Inside the boom

This looks good and also saves effort. You stand inside the boom to windward and counter the wind pressure with your back instead of with your hands. You can also reverse this trick by turning round and facing the wind, holding the boom in front of you. Another variation is to stand inside the boom to leeward of the sail.

Backwards somersault

You will already know this jump, and you can well imaging that it can only be used as the successful conclusion to a sailboard routine!